TRADING FATHERS

A MEMOIR

to Rich

TRADING FATHERS

FORGIVING DAD, EMBRACING GOD

KAREN RABBITT

WINEPRESS WP PUBLISHING

WinePress Publishing (PO Box 428, Enumclaw, WA 98022) functions only as book publisher. As such, the ultimate design, content, editorial accuracy, and views expressed or implied in this work are those of the author.

Only God knows exactly how everything happened. These are my memories, sometimes elaborated or compressed but never exaggerated. Many names and details have been changed to protect privacy.

Except where noted, Scripture is from the *Holy Bible, New International Version*®, NIV®, Copyright© 1973, 1978, 1984, by International Bible Society. Used by permission of Zondervan. All rights reserved.

Scripture references marked NASB are taken from the *New American Standard Bible*, © 1960, 1963, 1968, 1971, 1972, 1973, 1975, 1977 by The Lockman Foundation. Used by permission.

Scripture references marked KJV are taken from the authorized *King James Version* of the Bible.

ISBN 13: 978-1-57921-995-6
ISBN 10: 1-57921-995-0
Library of Congress Catalog Card Number: 2008907663

To Jerry, who demonstrates
Papa-God's love to me, every day.

And to Jenn, who has suffered because of my
sin and yet is willing to continue
the cycle of forgiveness.

Contents

PART III: ABUNDANCE BEYOND BELIEF

ACKNOWLEDGMENTS

Many thanks to . . .

Tom Hanlon. Your mentoring made the telling of this story possible.

Lin Johnson, Jane Rubietta, and Joyce Ellis, for the encouragement and opportunities of the Write-to-Publish Conference.

Richard Morris. You taught me the tools of creative nonfiction.

Dick and Ruth Foth and everyone else at Urbana Assembly of God (UAG) in the seventies. Your prayers and support restored my sanity.

Judy Husband, Mary Fisher, and Shereen Arulpragasam for the Friday afternoon prayer meetings.

Ron Baker, Sharon Chubbuck, Dean Davis-Smith, Lenita Epinger, Lorna Engels, Lee Ann Kelly, Jim and Nia Klein, Jim Linder, Ann Maronick, Bonnie Millikan, Elaine Mustain, Bev Stewart, Janet Welch, and Evelyn Zehr, in addition to many who wished to remain anonymous, who have prayed this book into existence. May God richly bless you all.

Elaine Mustain, Kay Warfel, Mary Siedenburg for your feedback, and Rob Siedenburg, for your feedback and editing. You've strengthened my belief in the value of the story.

Everyone at the Winepress Group, especially Athena Dean, Mike Owen, Tim Noreen, and Tammy Hopf. Thanks for a great job.

Soli Dei Gloria.

"Karen, Karen, Satan has asked to sift you as wheat. But I have prayed for you, Karen, that your faith may not fail. And when you have turned back, strengthen your brothers (and sisters)."
Luke 22:31, personalized, amplified

PART I
WILDERNESS
WANDERING

CHAPTER 1

My Father's Betrayal

Father," I prayed, "You know the darkness I feel from my parents. Be my light today. Honor this obedience." Jerry added his Amen. I massaged my throbbing forehead. We pulled to a stop at Route 34, just south of Halesburg. It was July 1997. My husband and I had driven north, through the cornfields of central Illinois, for our yearly visit to the family farm. I rummaged through the glove box, found two Tylenol Extra Strength, and washed them down.

I leaned my head against the seat back. "My father thinks I'm stupid because I grow flowers rather than tomatoes." I stared at the green cornstalks in the fields. "And has my mother ever asked me a question about my life?"

"Yeah, that's them," Jerry said. As he glanced at me, God's compassion shone in his gray eyes. In our twenty-five years together, Jerry had often seemed to me like the incarnation of Jesus. He even looked a little like I imagined Jesus to look: tall, with strong features and gentle hands.

"I don't think I've talked to them more than twice this year. And once was three weeks ago when I called to set up this visit." I ran my fingers through my short brown hair as I gazed at the mobile home park on the south edge of town, bigger now than I remembered. Jerry squeezed my shoulder. I smiled at him.

As the medication worked, the throbbing lessened. Passing the metal-sided grocery store downtown, my heart softened as I thought of the large family—eight children, plus my maternal grandmother who had lived with us—that my mother had fed from the proceeds of the small grain farm. They worked winter jobs, too. My father butchered beef at the processing plant; my mother cooked at the steak house. How many headaches had *they* endured?

In the last block of the business district, grayed plywood sheathed the windows of Laughlin's restaurant, where I had paid a quarter, handed to me by my mother every week after mass, for the Sunday *Chicago Tribune*. Threading my way through the tables full of townspeople eating their beef and gravy hot plates to the back room where the newspapers were stacked, I had worn my country poverty like a jacket of shame.

Just past the old restaurant, we turned right, passing classmates' houses on our way out of town. Across a railroad, just beyond a winding creek, the 180-acre farm began. Between the water and the road, a stand of pine trees grew. When I was in high school, my father had sheared off the back limbs to foil thieves who'd been stealing them for Christmas trees, but they looked full now.

We turned into the farmyard just past the orchard and pulled up near the old barnyard, where ducks, geese, and chickens had once pecked, but where grass and gardens now grew. Along the driveway, purple clusters of grapes hung heavy against broad green leaves. In my childhood the vines never bore fruit because of my father's herbicide overspray. Beyond the grapes, my parents, in their eighties, toiled among the tomatoes.

As we opened the car doors, my petite, white-haired mother straightened and waved, a watering can in her other hand. Such hard workers—I can respect that, I thought, returning the wave. My father, resting on a tubular metal kitchen chair that functioned as a garden bench, eyed us without lifting a hand. He's a tired old man—he can't hurt me.

He leaned over to grasp his gnarled wooden cane where it had fallen. Despite gripping the cane's rounded top with a shaky hand and using the chair's vinyl-covered back as a second support, he nearly stumbled as he stood on his arthritic knees, breathing heavily.

"Are you still nursing a forty-year hatred?" He wagged a crooked finger at me, his black eyes bright and hard behind his glasses. His unexpected rage felt like a ten-foot tsunami. I planted myself against the onslaught.

Leaning on her hoe, my mother watched us, silent. Behind me, Jerry grasped my shoulder. A few feet away, a cardinal called to its mate in the golden delicious apple tree. As I glanced at the wet black soil surrounding the tomatoes, trying to compose a response, I remembered a day before the time I started hating my father, a day more than forty years ago.

Was that the supper bell? Behind the red corncrib, near the field of green stalks that towered over me, I'd found just the right consistency of black mud I needed to make a pie for a tea party with my dollies.

As I turned to run to the house, my foot slipped in the goop. I sank into the mix of mud and poultry droppings up to the tops of my shoes. Finally, I wrestled myself out, but not without lying down to get some traction. My pants! Tears sprang to my eyes. Mom had just produced them from her stash of rummage sale finds that morning, when I had complained I didn't have anything to wear. She'd found another pair, too, but they were patched and had a big stain on the left leg. I'd whined to wear these today, even though they were good enough for a Sunday afternoon drive. "I'll be good," I'd said. "I'll keep them clean." Boy, would she be mad now! Our pigs kept themselves cleaner.

I ran into the kitchen. At the Formica table, everybody was waiting. Mom stood at the stove with her back to me, dishing up bean soup out of the deep well at the back of the stove. That meant they had already said grace. Grandma, feeding Henry at his highchair at the end of the table, didn't notice me, but my five older brothers and my sister stared. I felt even smaller than my almost four years. My mother turned toward the table to serve the soup, balancing three bowls. She nearly dropped them when she saw me. "You've ruined those good pants! What's the matter with you? Go wash up!"

"I got stuck in the mud," I said, my tears mingling with the black smears on my face.

"Yuk; you smell terrible," Fred said, holding his nose.

I felt dirty, and not just on the outside. I smelled bad, and I was bad. And my stomach was empty. I could smell the soup, with its bits of ham. If I went and washed up, I might lose out. For sure, there'd be no ham left. I hesitated, one muddy shoe on top of the other, biting a fingernail. My father, even though he had his back to me, seemed to sense I was still there, because he looked over his shoulder at me. His dark eyes looked tired. He must have seen the fear in my eyes because he said, "Go get cleaned up. I'll make sure there's enough left for you, Snooks. I'll even save a piece of ham."

I smiled really big at him, and with a little snort at Fred, turned to go to the bathroom. I heard my father say to him, "That's enough, now. She's just a little kid." He said that last part like it was okay to be little and not know enough to keep out of the mud. He came in from the fields almost as dirty as I was, so maybe I was okay, after all.

"No. I stopped hating you a long time ago," I said to my father. Small purple eggplants shone in the noonday sun. My parents were legendary gardeners. Next to the eggplants, the Brandywine tomatoes were starting to turn. Orange blossoms and gleaming fruit peeked out of the big zucchini leaves. A few feet away a bushel of onions awaited the cellar, and, down the middle of the apple trees, potato plants were blooming. The golden delicious apples, like most of the others, were still hard and bitter. Last week, however, when I phoned to say we were coming, Mom had said the Wolf River apples, an early variety, would be ready, and she'd bake a pie. I loved her pies. For days, I'd been imagining the taste of her flaky crust, enclosing the cinnamony richness of soft apples. Dessert on the farm never disappointed.

Nancy and Joe, my sister and brother-in-law, were out of town that weekend, or they would have joined us. They lived a few miles away, and, in addition to helping Mom and Dad, they raised their own vegetables at the farm. My other sibling who might have come for the day was Al, but his wife, Ann, had had surgery recently and wasn't able to travel. Another brother, Harold, lived in Illinois, too, but he was an institutionalized schizophrenic. My other brothers—Herb, Craig, Fred, and Henry, along with their families—were spread across the country. Today, it was just Dad, Mom, Jerry, and me.

Heart thumping, I forced myself to advance toward my father. He stiffened as I put my arm around his shoulders. I couldn't remember the last time I'd hugged him. Feeling his heat through the thin fabric of his dirty shirt took me back to the place where the hatred had begun.

It was an unusually warm October day, again wet from a rain. After lunch, my little brother, Henry, and I had been sent outside to play. I'd learned my lesson, so I was wearing an old stained pair of shorts that day, with a red flowered shirt. My frizzy brown hair stuck out at odd angles. We'd picked several hollyhock flowers and buds, and I was teaching Henry how to make "ladies."

"Here," I said, guiding his stubby fingers, "put the toothpick through the stem." I held the bud end as he jabbed the pick in.

"Now, put this flower on the other end of the toothpick." I held the open flower stem up for him to attach the two pieces. "Isn't that pretty?"

He just grinned. He didn't talk much yet. As we lined up a row of purple dolls, I felt like a real teacher. That's what I wanted to be when I grew up, ever since I'd met Mrs. Carter, the kindergarten teacher, last Saturday when Mom and I were at the grocery store. She had made me feel important, squatting down to my eye level, telling me about the picture books and toy kitchen area in her classroom.

I was imagining the pleasures of kindergarten play when Henry swept all our pretty ladies into a pile, crushing them. As I opened my mouth to yell at him, my father rounded the corner of the barn behind us, and his midafternoon shadow engulfed us both. I turned to tell him how Henry had ruined my little schoolroom, but I changed my mind when I saw the firm set of his face. He wasn't in any mood to listen to our little squabbles.

"Karen, come with me to the store," he said, holding out his hand. Gulping back my tears at Henry's destruction of my happy school scenario, I grabbed his hand and jumped up and down. He wasn't in a bad mood, after all. And he wanted to take me for a ride in the big Nash!

"Me, too!" Henry said.

"No, just Karen. You go inside. Now."

Henry began to cry, scrunching up his face in that silly way of his. I scowled at him. I got to do something he didn't. He swatted at me, missing my leg, before he ran toward the house. He'd tell Grandma how he didn't get to go with us and she'd stop sweeping the kitchen floor and read him a book. But I got to have my daddy all to myself. When you're one of eight kids, you don't get much time alone with your daddy, so even if you miss getting a book read to you, it's okay.

We walked, hand in hand, across the barnyard. I had to run, practically, to keep up. The chickens and ducks pecked nearby, but nobody else was around on this school day. It seemed odd Daddy would go to the store instead of Mom. If he went to town, it was to get parts or feed or seed. He'd take one of the boys for their young muscles. But Daddy knew what he was doing. I didn't question him. As if he could read my thoughts, he said, "It's too wet to get the picker in the fields, and Mom needs bread for supper."

"Can we get ice cream?" We'd had the treat for my recent birthday.

"We'll see." I knew that meant to be quiet and good and maybe, even probably, my request would be granted. "Get your shoes on."

"Should I change my shorts?"

"No, they're fine."

I ran to the garage where I'd left my shoes and buckled them on quickly. I hopped into the frayed front seat of the Nash, where I'd never ridden alone. Mom always rode in the front passenger seat, with Henry between her and Dad, now that he was the baby. Today, I had it all to myself. I was the special one today. The dark interior of the car smelled like the King Arthur tobacco Daddy smoked in his wooden pipe. I struggled to close the door as the engine rumbled. I loved the sound, like a lion roaring. After I got the heavy door shut, I sat on my legs to see out the window better. The tires crunched on the gravel of the driveway as we pulled away.

"Pretty hot for October, isn't it," he said.

"Yeah." I couldn't remember any other Octobers, even though it was my birthday month. I remembered the big chocolate cake Mom had baked, with my name written in yellow icing. I got to eat a big piece, even before dinner. Then I got to eat another piece afterward—even better with the ice cream!

We pulled into a diagonal parking space in front of Cross's grocery store. I scrambled across the wide seat to get out Daddy's side of the car. He lifted me up on the high sidewalk and stepped up himself. The little grocery displayed all kinds of good food, but Daddy headed right for the bread aisle. Picking up a Honey Wheat, he turned toward the front of the store, not stopping at the ice cream freezer.

"Daddy, you said we could get some ice cream."

"I said we'd see. I see it's not on sale." He frowned at me as he pulled out some coins from his trousers and handed them to Mrs. Cross.

"How are you, today, Alice?" he said.

"Pretty hot. Okay, though." She handed him a dime change.

"But I've been good," I said, tugging on his sleeve.

Mrs. Cross smiled at me. "You are a good girl, aren't you?"

Daddy unhooked my hand from his sleeve and pulled me through the door. "We can't afford it. Now be quiet about it." He lifted me into the car.

I was crying by then. "We'll see" was almost a promise, and you were supposed to keep promises.

He sped toward home, but when we approached our driveway, he kept going.

"Where are we going?" I said.

"Out to see if the fields are still wet. Come over here. You can drive."

I dried my tears on my faded shirt, scooted onto his lap, and grasped the big wheel. I was driving. Wait until Henry hears about this. It's even better than ice cream!

When we got to the corner, half a mile north of our house, I slowly turned the big wheel to the left. After we crossed the creek flowing out of our back fields, Daddy helped me turn onto the rough ground of the half-picked cornfield. He stopped the big Nash behind the tall stalks. Just over the fence, a spring bubbled. When my big brothers took me to play with them at the creek, we usually got a drink from the spring. Maybe we'd walk down the farm road that forded the waterway to see whether there were any fish in the creek. I loved playing in the water, and I wasn't allowed to go to the creek by myself, so that would be fun. Just me and my Daddy. He never took me out just by myself. We'd probably get a drink first. I was thirsty. I could almost taste the fresh water.

But we didn't drink from the bubbling spring. Daddy didn't show me the shiny fish in the water. Instead, he held me in silence for what seemed like a long time, his grip on me slowly tightening. What was he doing? Why weren't we getting a drink? Abruptly, he laid me out on the car seat, squashing the bread on the seat beside us with my head, and began to touch me in ways that I had never imagined. I couldn't breathe. I wanted to scream, but I couldn't breathe. I stared in horror at his expressionless eyes, fixed on me—but not in love.

Finally, he let me go. I scrambled to the passenger door and pressed against it, even though the armrest dug into my side. I hardly noticed. I stared out the window at the bubbling spring. I felt dry as a desert.

He restarted the car. "Now, you get back over here and sit on my lap, or I'll do it again." He grabbed my arm and yanked me back onto his thigh.

"Don't tell Mommy. This is our little secret. I did it so you'll let your husband play with you, too." Play? Not like any play I knew. I never wanted a husband if that's what they did to you.

"What about the bread?" I whispered. It lay half-mashed in the corner.

"We'll say we dropped it."

When my father pulled up in front of the garage, before he even turned off the ignition, I bolted out the car door.

He hollered after me. "Here, take the bread in."

I dared not disobey. Though out of his reach, I was still inside his authority. I ran back to the driver's side and grabbed it out of his hand, careful not to touch his fingers. The chickens pecked around my feet as I hurried into the house. My mother, weeding the garden, waved. I didn't stop. Dropping the bread on the kitchen table, I escaped to my bedroom. My heart raced as I ran up the back stairs, crying. Annie, my big dolly, was leaning in the corner. Wiping my nose on my sleeve, I took her over my knees, pulled down her pants, and hit her bare bottom. "You nasty girl. You've been playing with George again. He's a bad boy."

Throwing Annie aside, I picked up my baby Cathy doll, and curled on the bed, hugging her to my chest. I squeezed my legs together and rubbed my eyes. My father had looked at me through his bifocals. Maybe rubbing my eyes would get that image out of my head. My whole body felt empty, as if he'd gutted my insides. Through the open window,

I could hear the grinder out at the machine shed. He was probably sharpening hoes to go help Mom in the garden. Usually I liked to stand at the entrance to watch the sparks fly, but now I never wanted to watch the sparks again. The smallest one would set fire to this wilderness inside me.

CHAPTER 2

TWO TRUTHS

Closing my mind's eye, I reoriented myself to 1997, in the garden on the farm with my husband and parents. My father jerked his shoulder from my arm. I stiffened. I was a psychotherapist. When my clients raged, I required them to take a timeout. But this was my father's turf. Besides, I wondered what had brought on this intensity. My mother stood by, still leaning on her hoe, still saying nothing, expressionless. A rotten onion lay near my feet.

He narrowed his eyes. "I'm sorry I took indecent liberties with you when you were a child. I've got guns in there if you want blood." Nodding his head towards the house, he pointed an index finger to his forehead. A few strands of thin gray hair fell against his finger.

"No," I began, but he cut me off. I was going to say, "Jesus shed his, you don't need to shed yours."

"You wouldn't even be here if I wasn't oversexed. Mother told me this morning that I forced myself on her the night you were conceived. She says I raped her." He glared at me.

I couldn't believe it. Not that I couldn't believe he'd raped my mother—that I believed. And I wasn't even surprised my mother had only now, forty-six years later, confronted him. Instead, his trampling of the first rule of dysfunctional families—"Don't talk about the real issues, in this case, rape and sexual abuse"—is what left my jaw hanging. But I closed my mouth as an adolescent self-doubt flashed through my mind: What justifies my existence? In junior college, I'd often wandered the streets, wondering why I was alive. Before I found myself in Jesus, I felt worthless.

"Well, that explains a lot." If I was a product of rape, no wonder I'd questioned my right to life.

Jerry squeezed my shoulder. I covered his hand with mine. I knew he was praying.

"This morning, Mother tells me she should have left me years ago." As my father spoke, he turned away, marching toward the house. I followed him, hoping he would calm down and for the first time we could talk seriously about the real issues in our relationship. He stopped and turned to me halfway across the driveway, raising a fist.

"You're only in the will because that's what Mother wants. If she dies before me, I can do what I want with the money." Turning toward the house again, he threw his last jab over his shoulder, "If I'm not forgiven, you won't get anything."

Just before he reached the steps, I laid my hand on his back, but my touch didn't stop his momentum. "You are forgiven," I said.

He wiped a tear as he moved away from my hand, but he said nothing as he slid open the family room door. He continued through the kitchen and the old parlor and disappeared through the curtained entrance into their bedroom. If he'd had a door to slam, I would have felt it in the family room, where I had stopped, staring after him. Mom and Jerry entered the open door behind me.

I touched my mother's shoulder. "You've had a bad morning." If my father wouldn't talk, perhaps she would.

"Yes. Maybe it'll be better now." As she spoke, she turned toward her overstuffed lounge chair. That was all she said. I wasn't surprised. I was amazed she'd confronted my father at all. My mother avoided conflict like most people avoid rattlesnakes. Jerry followed, sitting on the orange and green crocheted afghan thrown over the sofa.

As I took a seat next to Jerry, my thoughts raced: It'll be better now that my father has had his rage? I don't think so. What provoked her confrontation about the rape, now? How did her naming the rape translate into his angry tirade at me? How did my mother know the rape was my conception? Was that the only time he had raped her? My parents had married in February 1938. My oldest brother was born seven months later. I was the seventh of their eight children.

The silence emanating from the bedroom surrounded us. *Arizona Highways* magazines lay scattered on dusty tables made of varnished tree trunk slices. My gaze wandered to the Hummel Madonna, a gift from my mother's sister's trip to Germany, ensconced in the stone fireplace my father had built. The cinnamon apple fragrance from the pies sitting on the kitchen table wafted into the family room, but for once I wasn't thinking about food. Jerry squeezed my hand. The sun shone through the wide south windows. If only the light could illuminate this tangled web.

"How are your orchids doing?" my mother asked Jerry, settling into her chair. He grew orchids under bright lights in an insulated room he'd built in our basement.

"Oh, good. The oncidium are full of flowers."

I understood his following my mother in her foray into oblivion. I didn't jump into the fray either. My father didn't make any sense, and my mother wouldn't talk at all. This is why we don't visit, I thought. They are too crazy-making. Is my father loading a gun, while his wife and son-in-law discuss orchids? I can leave. I don't have to sit here talking about orchids, as if threatening suicide were normal behavior.

As I walked to the door, neither of them asked where I was going. Their smoothing-over talk faded as I opened the screen and stepped into the fresh air. I wandered through the vegetable gardens until I found myself behind the corncrib. Deep, dusty ruts remained where I used to play in the mud. I sat among the weeds that grew next to the building, and leaned against the red siding. The warm wind caressed my face. Something felt crazy about my father's monologue. I would get no inheritance if I didn't forgive him? If I wanted blood, he would kill himself? Was he aiming the gun at his forehead right now? I stared at the corn that concealed the creek a quarter mile away. The old path to the water was gone now, plowed by the tenant farmer for a few more rows. I would get lost if I tried to escape to the soothing stream.

Oversexed? In his mind, the molestation was not a choice or even an irresistible impulse; it was an unchangeable personality trait. *This is the conviction you've prayed for. It's as much responsibility as he's going to take.* A Voice I'd learned to listen to broke through my confusion. Yes, in spite of the surreal quality of the interaction, the monologue in the garden was an answer to prayer—to both my long-term prayer that my father would take responsibility for his sin, and to this morning's prayer for light in the midst of their darkness. But we saw the abuse very differently. In his view, he was the victim rather than the perpetrator, ready to kill himself because he thought I wanted revenge. But I didn't need retribution—not anymore. I wanted an honest, warm relationship with a father.

Then I thought: Mom isn't concerned. She's discussing orchids. She knows he won't kill himself—the suicide threat is his typical power play. Okay. I made myself breathe. Gulping deep drafts of fresh air, I dragged myself back toward my father's house of perpetual subterranean conflict. In spite of professional training in conflict resolution, I could not force the issue. My father had said his piece. He was done talking to me.

When I opened the screen door to the family room, my parents were talking in the corner. Jerry was leafing through *Arizona Highways*, looking at images of the desert. As I sat next to him, I overheard my father say to my mother, "I'm sorry I made a scene." I leaned against Jerry's solid strength.

Each took a seat and turned to us, smiling brightly.

My mother said, "Has it been hot down your way?"

The visit then proceeded like every other, full of talk about family members' health, the growing number of great-grandchildren, and the quality of the corn and soybean crop that year. At lunch, we sat at the Formica table with its padded chairs that my mother and I had shopped for thirty years before. We ate the overcooked chuck roast, with potatoes and carrots, finishing off the meal with warm apple pie, as rich as ever. Food: my mother's currency of love and pleasure that blunted pain. No wonder I was forty pounds overweight.

After my father's retirement from farming, he'd developed a flea-market business of cutting and polishing semiprecious stones, specializing in opals. Only when he gave me four of the fiery stones later that morning did he reference our relationship: "You haven't gotten as much as the other kids have because of our troubles."

I mused on his meaning. Because we had not visited often, we didn't get presents? He had punished me for the conflict through withholding his gifts? I thought punishment more likely, given his vindictive nature.

Whatever he meant, his description intrigued me. I wondered whether he intended the evocation of the Irish multiyear family war—the Troubles. Our Catholic-Protestant conflict was part of our trouble, but only a small part. His coercion, of which this morning was only one example, continued to feel oppressive. Though I'd forgiven him the early abuse, I still couldn't trust him. I'd learned to put on Holy Spirit armor—the breastplate of Jesus' righteousness, the helmet of God's promise of wholeness—before I opened the door to that room where my father waited. His jabs no longer penetrated my heart, but the confusions of that day lodged in my spirit.

Only when I woke in my own bed the next morning did I sort out the confusion: I should be glad my father was a sexual abuser because I was created when he raped my mother. Born of a "husband's will," and I should be glad of it! Though I hadn't been so sure in early adulthood, I was glad to be alive. I could not, however, be glad of the price of my conception.

But I was grateful for my father's intensity. I was glad for the slightest breaking of the "No talk" rule.

When my father had raged yesterday morning, his real, though convoluted, pain had come through. And I felt sorry for him. I picked up my journal and wrote:

> Normally, when you hurt someone and you want to repent, you say you're sorry and "Is there any way I can make it up to you?" He was saying he was sorry for horrible things, but then seeking to justify himself. Poor guy—he doesn't have much of a clue about how to be intimate, but he did want to hear my forgiveness, I think. He knows only force and coercion to get what he wants.

When my father was in the grip of his anger, only his tears expressed his pain. That morning, when I realized that my hatred had hurt him, I wrote an apology. "Please forgive me for those years of hatred. God doesn't give me the prerogative to hate, no matter what."

A week later, on the back of the yellow lined sheet on which I'd written my apology, he wrote: "How hard it is to be humble, but 'I forgive.'"

I thought: how did this get to be about how hard forgiveness is for him? But I was done trying to make him see my point of view. All I knew was that he forgave my hatred; I had forgiven his abuse. Jesus died for my sin. Jesus died for my father's sin. We will both give an account, under the grace and mercy of the cross, in the last act of this long story God is telling.

But forgiveness and reconciliation are two different things. Forgiveness means giving up the right to revenge; reconciliation means regaining trust. Trust is built by listening. My father didn't listen.

Though my trust in my father remained broken, my trust in Father-God had grown wide and long and deep by 1997. In the forty years between the abuse in the cornfield and the revelation in the garden, I had found, in the Father of Jesus, a new Father. In fact, I often called him Papa to express my trust in his deep love. Through the confusing wilderness of my childhood and early adulthood, he had walked with me into a rich landscape. By this visit in 1997, daffodils, roses, and lilies were all in bud.

But the wilderness was hell. On the schoolyard I overreacted to small snubs. In high school my self-consciousness paralyzed me. In college I wondered whether I'd ever stop crying. At twenty, when I met Jesus and his Father, I was overjoyed, but the battles were just beginning. In early adulthood, I was hospitalized twice for psychotic episodes, taking strong medications to quiet my fears. After those days of terror, however, I heard God: *Karen, dear, you have deeply rooted weeds in your heart. Let me pull them.*

Before those emotional breakdowns at twenty-three and twenty-five years old, I had not seriously addressed the abuse effects—distrust, anxiety, perfectionism, depression, and, underlying them all, shame. After the second breakdown, I began a journey into emotional and spiritual wholeness. I fought the most intense battles from 1977 to 1987. What was hardest was what I needed most—to trust God's goodness after my trust in my father's goodness had so betrayed me.

Many of us were reared by difficult fathers, to a lesser or greater degree. Others' fathers were absent, through death or desertion. We long for a good father. We long to lean our heads against a father's strong shoulder. We long to walk on the beach, waves lapping at our feet, hand in hand with a father. We need a father willing to confront our disobedience. Many of us cannot imagine a father who is tender-hearted toward us and committed to our best interests.

We have a Papa-God, however, who wants to father us into wholeness. Even if our fathers fail to walk hand in hand with us, our Forever Father wants to walk beside us through all our confusion, leading us to the abundant life Jesus promised.

It was years, though, before abundance even occurred to me as a possibility. Through my childhood and well into my adulthood, I stumbled through the days, confused and lonely.

CHAPTER 3

LONELY AND AFRAID

Who wants to go to the blackboard to work addition problems?" Mrs. Rand, my first grade teacher, asked.

Waving my hand, I said, "I do, I do!" Working at the board was like being the teacher. Besides, I liked to show off what I knew.

"All right, Karen, you and Paula and Glen," she said, pointing to each of us.

I jumped up and ran to the board in the back of the room. The other children turned in their desks to watch. I rubbed the smooth, cool chalk against my hand—a tool that usually only the teacher touched.

"Now, children, write two plus three." She spoke from the front of the room.

Finishing my "3," I sneaked a glance at Paula's "3," next to me. Mine looked better, more like the model ones displayed above the board.

"Now, write the answer."

Shaping my "5," I noticed Paula staring at her problem. Glen had written a "6." Just then, a gathering pressure in my bladder asserted itself. I can't ask to go to the bathroom from here, can I? Nobody else ever had. Wouldn't Mrs. Rand be mad? I'd already gotten in a lot of trouble with my father doing bad things to me, so adults scared me. They could really hurt you. I didn't know why he'd touched me like that and made me feel all dirty inside, but maybe, if I was a really good girl, nobody would hurt me again. The hallway door was right next to me, but I didn't dare run out without permission, so I squeezed hard. Leaving without asking could get a spanking.

However, maybe Mrs. Rand would be nice. At the beginning of the school year, a month ago, she'd noticed I couldn't say my *r* right. I said it like a *w*. She referred me to the speech teacher, who came on Tuesdays and took me down to the basement of the two-story red brick schoolhouse in the middle of our little village. I liked hearing my voice on the recorder. My big brother, Harold, who slept in the room next to mine, had a tape recorder. I loved to see the big reels wind around while my voice was coming out of the speakers. I didn't sound the same at all. At first I didn't know it was my voice. I was sure something was wrong with the recorder, but Harold said that's what I sounded like. So, anyway, when I heard myself on the speech teacher's tape recorder, I didn't embarrass myself by saying it wasn't me. I already knew it sounded different. I was embarrassed about my speech problem, but the teacher helped me. Like how to say "rabbit" instead of "wabbit."

At the blackboard, I clasped my knees together and scrunched up my face. Billy, in the closest desk, whispered, "What's wrong with you?"

That did it. I started crying and leaking and getting red all at once. My pink corduroy pants darkened as the warm liquid trickled down my legs. Everybody started laughing. I hung my head. Hot tears fell off my cheeks, splatting on the polished pine floor. A blue jay squawked outside our window. He was probably telling his bird friends how stupid I was. My chest felt heavy, like somebody was pushing on me.

But Mrs. Rand came to the back of the room and put a hand on my shoulder. "That's enough, now, children," she said. She walked me to the adjacent cloakroom and handed me a dry pair of pants. I beamed at her before running to the bathroom to change. When I got back to the class, she must have given them a good talking-to, because nobody said a word to me about it. However, my face still burned, and having hung the wet pants on my hook in the cloakroom, I was afraid they would stink. In reading group, later, I kept losing my place. When Mrs. Rand called on me to read out loud, twice I had to ask her where we were. She just smiled at me, though, when she told me the page.

Later that day when I got off the yellow school bus after the hour ride home, I glanced around for my father, relieved when I didn't see him. Herb and Harold, out in the pasture, were herding the cows home to milk. They'd ridden the mile home from school on Herb's old motorcycle. Al, Nancy, Craig, and Fred piled out of the bus behind me, running into the house. Our bus ride took an hour because the route covered forty miles, stopping at the farms to drop kids off, sometimes at half-mile-long lanes. Being almost the last on the route was good in the morning, though. We could sleep an hour later than the other country kids.

When the school bus screeched to a dusty halt at the edge of the hedge that lined the road, Henry had jumped up from where he was playing in the gravel driveway and run toward me, clutching a yellow car in his fist. In his other arm, he was holding my baby doll, Ruthie, new last year. Its orange-checked dress was dirty, and the white ribbon was loose. One dolly was my only Christmas present. I loved that new dolly smell. Ruthie's new smell had faded, but

Christmas would come again in a few months, and I longed for that sweet aroma. In the meantime, I had only four dollies. I kept them in my room, where he wasn't allowed.

"What are you doing with my dolly?" I shouted as I grabbed it out of his hands. What else had he gotten into? Were my others all right?

"You left it on the chair." He grabbed at her dress, but I held on. The skirt tore out of the bodice. I cried for the second time that day. First wetting my pants, and now tearing up my newest baby doll's only dress.

"Now look what you've done. Let me have her. She's mine!" I said.

He let go, running toward the house. He'll tell on me, probably. He'd sniffle and whimper and tell Grandma I'd been mean to him. She'd hold him and give him some sweet cinnamon applesauce, like she always did. He was her favorite. She helped him take out the table scraps to the compost heap, too. That was supposed to be his job, like drying the dishes was mine. She never helped me dry the dishes.

Instead of going inside, I ran to my hideout under the front porch, ducking in between the broken wood slats. I sat on a wadded-up rag in the dirt, holding my doll to my chest, drying my tears with the torn skirt. Mom was probably too busy to listen to what happened anyway, and she'd just say if

I had shared my dolly that wouldn't have happened. She'd be mad about my wetting my pants. They'd dried without stinking too much because Mrs. Rand had opened the window in the cloakroom, so I wore them home, but they still had a stain. Maybe Mom wouldn't be mad I'd wet them, but she'd think I was a dummy not to ask to go to the bathroom. Mrs. Rand had told me after class that it was okay to ask anytime if I needed to use the restroom. That's what she called it, "restroom." She was a teacher, and she lived in town instead of on a gravel road in the country. I was going to call it "restroom," too.

That night I snuggled into bed, pulling the ragged quilt around my shoulders, sinking my head into the homemade feather pillow. My sister wouldn't come upstairs for hours. Chewing on a lock of my hair, I thought about how the kids had made fun of me. My chest felt heavy again, like Billy, the fattest boy in my class, was sitting on it. I saw each one of their laughing faces. Why did they laugh? The weight felt heavier on my chest as I began to cry. My nose stopped up. I held myself and rolled back and forth.

Then the thought came to me: They were the bad boys and girls, not me. Mrs. Rand was mad at them, not me. I blew my nose on the sheet. Pulling myself up, I fluffed the pillow and leaned against it. My chest expanded as my anger rose. Just like the whole class was right there in my bedroom, I told them all to line up. I imagined Billy laughing and Glen smirking, and Paula looking a little scared. Then, just inside my mind, I went down the line, spanking each one of them, hard. With each swat, I felt better, until my whole body felt warm and really good. I got to be the big girl who could decide who got hurt. That power felt like a refreshing rain falling on my desert.

I didn't tell my mother about wetting my pants, and she didn't ask about the stain. She probably missed it, with all the other clothes. She washed every Monday, in the damp cellar, using the Easy washing machine. We used less water than an automatic, she said. Each tub of hot water cleaned three loads. First we'd wash whites, then coloreds, and then work clothes. During the spring and fall fieldwork, we'd wash two loads of work clothes before changing the water. After each load's agitation, we lifted the hot garments into the open spinner, using a thick stick if they were the first scalding hot water load. I often leaned against the hot washer, losing self-consciousness, staring into the moving clothes, letting my body vibrate as the agitator swished, and the spinner spun. Hours of my childhood were spent in this reverie at the washer, escaping the various snubs that penetrated my soul, coming, as they did, on top of my father's betrayal.

On the playground one day in second grade, my classmate Paula and I were playing dolls when a group of girls walked by, their full cancan slips swishing under their voluminous skirts.

"Are you friends with Ruth Ann?" Paula said, staring after the leader of the pack.

"Yeah, I guess so. Are you?" After all, we went to her cousin's house and played in the pool all day when we were in kindergarten.

"I don't know. I've never played with her. Have you been to her house?"

"Yeah, I played dolls at her house. We had root beer floats, too!"

"Let's go play dolls with them now." They had gathered on the grass a few feet away from us, arranging themselves around Ruth Ann, who was holding up a Betsy McCall doll. I had lots of the paper Betsy dolls, which I had cut out of the back of Grandma's *McCall's Magazine,* but I didn't have the real doll, which had come out last year. Ruth Ann spoke in a high-pitched voice. "Hi, I'm Betsy. I'm the teacher. Today we're going to play all day."

I laughed as Paula and I sat down near them.

Without looking away from her doll, Ruth Ann said, "That's Karen. I can tell by her silly giggle."

The girls with her laughed, along with Paula. My cheeks burned as if I'd been slapped. What was wrong with how I laughed? Turning on my heel, I ran toward the building, clutching my baby doll. Maybe I could hide in the restroom.

That day I learned that not only adults or groups of kids, but also individual kids could hurt me. Like my confusing father, who saved a piece of ham for me one day and molested me the next, the social rejection from the queen bee confused me after our earlier friendship. I didn't think about the confusion when I was a kid, but I know my emotional life felt like one big tangled mess, with nobody who understood. It never occurred to me to talk about it. Who to? Besides, I had no words to describe my feelings. I did try once, though, to talk about the deepest pain. It was the summer before that second grade incident with the queen bee.

My father and brothers were going on an all-day trip to visit relatives, and they wanted me to go with them. My sister was spending the day with a friend. Mom was staying home. I didn't know why she wasn't going, but I wasn't going if she wasn't. I felt a little bit safer if I was close to her.

Fred noticed me standing in the doorway, biting my fingernail. "Are you coming with us?" They were gathering at the car, still the old Nash.

"No." Leaning on the wall, I rubbed my bare foot against my other leg.

Opening the door, he gestured to the back seat. "Oh, come on, it'll be fun."

"No, I don't want to." I turned away just as my father came up behind me.

He took my arm. "Get your shoes on."

"I don't want to go." I wrestled free of his hand. I guess my mother had been listening to this exchange, because she stepped out of the kitchen then.

"She doesn't have to go if she doesn't want to."

As they pulled out of the drive, my mother turned to me. "Why didn't you go?"

"They're all boys." I picked at a loose thread in my brown shirt. I sat on the floor and picked up my baby doll.

"They're your brothers—and your Daddy."

I can't tell. Daddy will spank me. He hit really hard. I unbuttoned my dolly's dress and pulled it off. Then I pulled her little pink undies off. My mother stared at me. I stared at my dolly, sucking in air. Mother waited. I took a deep breath. "Daddy took me to the cornfield when I was four and took down my pants and did bad things to me." I knew I'd get in trouble, but I couldn't hold in the secret any longer. I rubbed at a dirty smear on my dolly's bottom.

"But you were so young, and it was a long time ago." She sat down, picked up the folded newspaper, and laid it in her lap. She made no move to put me in her lap.

Feeling utterly alone, I climbed the back stairway to my room, dragging the naked doll. I threw myself on my bed and pulled the covers up over my head. Why did I tell? She doesn't care. Nobody cares.

Even before the abuse and the telling, though, I felt emotionally neglected. When I imagine my mother, I see her either behind the newspaper or busy in the kitchen. With eight children, I'm sure she was often exhausted, but that doesn't explain her unresponsiveness to emotional need. I don't know much of my mother's own childhood, but she, too, must have received little empathy. In fact, one time my mother pointed out my grandmother's lack of warmth. Looking at a photo of a young Grandma, I said to my mother, "She's not smiling."

"Have you ever seen her smile?" my mother responded. Even that comment was an unusual attention to emotion. My mother was a hard-working German woman who did her duties. But those duties did not include emotional warmth. I do not remember my mother ever kissing me, and I was an adult visiting home before she even hugged me hello.

On the day I told, I should have known seeking her comfort was useless. I'd already experienced her emotional distance on an August day before the abuse, in the summer of 1955.

On that hot day, everybody else was working in the fields. Even Fred and Craig, at six and eight years old, could help walk beans, cutting out the button weeds that would contaminate the harvest. On the farm, even elementary-age boys were assets. Henry was still a baby, though, so he crawled around inside. Mom and Grandma were canning, adding heat and humidity to the kitchen air. Three wooden bushel baskets full of Roma tomatoes covered the table. Grandma peeled, while Mom packed them into Mason jars and put them in the water bath. I tried to help peel, but the tomatoes kept slipping out of my hands. After the fifth one splattered on the floor, I was sent outside.

A mourning dove cooed as I headed out the back door to the strawberry patch to look for a sweet treat. My brown shorts and blue plaid blouse stuck to my skin. But not only were there no berries, the heat had dried the plants into brown crisps. I wish I could go down to the creek by myself, I thought. I sat on the grass next to the patch, looking for something to do.

A light breeze nudged the tops of the maples. I wanted to climb the tall trees, but without help, I couldn't reach the first branch. Then I noticed the ducks quacking around their feeder in the barnyard. Jumping up and running toward them, I called, "Here, ducky, ducky." I wanted to pet their smooth feathers, but they ignored me, scattering around my feet.

Then I saw the grain elevator, rising to the roof of the red-slatted corncrib, twenty feet high. It was an open trough with a foot-wide conveyer belt to which three-inch tall paddles were affixed every few inches. The elevator beckoned, promising a cooling breeze if I climbed it to the top. With nobody to stop me, I stepped into the still conveyance. Holding on to the sides as I climbed, I easily reached the edge of the crib's roof, where I clambered onto the shingles. But before I could stand up to enjoy the breeze, I rolled off the steep edge. I crashed into the ground on my left side, onto a two-foot pile of decomposed corn, two feet from a parked cultivator. I shuddered as I imagined myself impaled on its tines. I picked myself up, and staggered across the barnyard toward the kitchen. Before I reached it, I managed to brush off some of the wet dirt and corn residue. My knee bled and the left side of my hand was turning blue. Tears ran down my hot cheeks.

"What happened to you?" my mother asked, glancing up from the boiling pot of tomato jars. "How'd you get corn in your hair?"

I felt for the kernels and picked them off. "I fell off the crib." I climbed onto the stool next to the sink and ran water over my bruised hand, using my undamaged hand to splash water on my bleeding knee.

"You what?! What were you doing up there?" She lifted the hot jars from the bath to the counter, setting them on a rack to cool. Grandma, her apron soaked with the juice running off the table, looked up from peeling tomatoes. Henry howled from the other room, and she went to investigate.

"I don't know." Wiping my hands and knee on a stained kitchen towel, I turned to go.

"Are you all right? I'm in the middle of canning."

"Yeah."

I went back outside through the enclosed porch, where dusty outerwear and boots lined the walls, heading for the flower gardens across the driveway. I wanted to pop some balloon flower buds. Just like balloons, they made a satisfying pop when they were pinched. But their budding time was over. As I yanked at one of the balloon plants, I noticed the smell of the oriental lilies, their big white blooms almost at my nose level. Inhaling, I lay down in the grassy path, staring at the clouds. My knee had stopped bleeding, but my hand still hurt and my hip was beginning to ache.

CHAPTER 4

ADOLESCENT ANGST
INTENSIFIED

In my family, I got little attention from my parents unless I was bleeding or broken. If I cried, "I'll give you something to cry about" was a common admonition used to shut me up. In that emotional wilderness, my tears dried up, leaving a salty residue. At the time, I couldn't have said how thirsty I was for someone, anyone, to hold me and say, "I understand how you feel. Your sadness and anger make sense." Looking back, putting words to feelings, I know I believed that if my mother didn't take my pain seriously, who would? A companion question to "If my father can't be trusted, who can?"

One evening when I was eight years old, my mother was gone to a church meeting. My brothers were milking the cows across the barnyard. Grandma had already retired for the night in her room at the top of the stairs. My father walked through the living room where I was reading *Heidi* and grabbed my hand. "Come help me bank the fire." To keep burning through the winter nights, the coal furnace required daily attention.

"Do I have to?" Not only was I reading, but last week, he'd made me help him undress by pulling his pants off while he sat on his bed. I'd gotten out of there as fast as I could.

"Yes, you have to." The fake smile he gave me didn't fool me. Menace lay beneath.

My father pulled me along, through the kitchen, to the dark hallway past the bathroom that led to the cellar. My heart raced, but I didn't try to pull away. That would have gotten a spanking. He brooked no disobedience.

We descended the stairs into the dank cellar where Mother's rows of canned apples and pickles sat on the shelves below. He still had hold of my hand. I had listened at the top of those stairs the other day when my father used the razor strap on my brother's bare bottom. My brother's sobs had echoed off the walls.

He pulled me over to the hot furnace and hoisted me onto a ledge that ran around the perimeter of the dark space. From the pile heaped in the corner, he shoveled three loads of coal into the firebox. Then he turned to me, trembling on the high ledge. When he had finished touching me, he pulled my pants up and swung me down onto the floor full of coal dust. "Now this is our little secret, remember?" My bare feet turned black as I ran toward the stairs. Inside I felt as dirty as the dust. How could I forget to keep the secret? Nobody cared, anyway.

The years from eight to twelve passed in a blur. Like most children of trauma, I remember little, either bad or good. I know I went to Catholic mass every Sunday morning. Though it would be years before I really understood God's fatherhood, the little steepled church was a genuine sanctuary. Catholics know the value of using all our senses in worship. Recently, Jerry and I walked into a Greek Orthodox church for an open house, and the smell of the incense transported me to those early Catholic days of mystery and majesty. Father Wright would walk down the aisle toward the altar, swinging the smoking censer of fragrant incense on special holy days. The arched stained glass windows glowed, the choir behind us in the loft sang the great hymns of the faith, and, for an hour on Sunday mornings, I felt clean.

On those Sunday mornings, we looked pretty good. We were there as a family, we took communion, and we knew the catechism. We paid our bills and lived in the same house all the time I grew up. In fact, at my father's funeral, that's what a childhood classmate said to me: "What a good family." And, in some important ways, we were a functional family. We worked together in the garden that fed us all. We raised the usual Midwestern fare: tomatoes, peppers, cucumbers, cabbage, peas, lima beans, lettuce, green beans and corn; and the unusual: peanuts and tobacco. We gathered eggs and killed and cleaned poultry for Sunday dinners. The fruit orchard my parents had planted when they moved to the farm in Halesburg in the early forties yielded bushels of apples, along with plums and apricots. Grandma made gallons of applesauce, standing at the electric stove, mashing the soft apples with the potato masher. Dad hunted and fished for protein. Pheasant and duck, deer and goose—fare that was exotic in the city was common on our table.

My father was a talented man, able to butcher a cow, skin a deer, clean a fish, spot a fox, and build anything he wanted to—from a shed to a stone fireplace. A natural mechanical engineer, he could fix any farm equipment, from tractors to planters to combines. My mother was a time and motion expert, running an organized eleven-member household.

By the time I was in sixth grade, in 1963, the three oldest boys were in the military, but Mother cooked large meals for many years. Having regularly cooked for only two or three myself, I can't imagine the work of daily meals for up to eleven people. But she did the work and also held down outside jobs in local restaurants. She packed lunches for us, too: Honey Wheat bread layered with baloney and oleo, lined up on the counters, ready for us to pick up on our way to the school bus.

For a few weeks in the spring and fall, during the planting or harvest, Dad and the boys worked eighteen hours a day. Summer work included cultivating the fields. A tractor pulled a wheeled implement, with many hoes attached in rows to loosen the dirt and cut out weeds. Two to three times during the summer we baled hay. On the whole, my brothers and father worked the small farm themselves, but during hay time my father hired three or four young men to help with the work.

In the field, haying requires someone to drive the tractor pulling the baler and wagon, along with two men to stack the forty-five pound bales on the hayrack. Back at the barn, two or three guys were needed to stack the bales in the second floor loft as they came off the elevator that lifted them from the full wagons. They worked through the heat of the day, which in July in northern Illinois could be ninety-five degrees with ninety percent humidity.

My role in farm work was typical for a girl in the early sixties. I helped my mother make and deliver baloney salad sandwiches and cold Kool-Aid for the boys. We would eat with them in the hot field, surrounded by the smell of dried alfalfa, and sometimes I'd get a little teasing attention from the hired hands.

Then Mr. Edwards came to town to teach my sixth grade class. Hungry for male nurturance, I played up to that young first-year teacher. I called him at home in the evenings for help with homework. I often approached him in class. And I dreamed about kissing him. He looked a little like Abraham Lincoln, whose biography I read that year. I was in love. He, in turn, encouraged my adulation. One day in the classroom, when I took my paper to him, he asked, "Do you still love me?"

My face heated up. "Yes."

How ever over-the-top that teacher may have been, he attended to me. He never touched me inappropriately. My father, except when he wanted to take advantage of me, rarely made eye contact or talked to me. Occasionally, after dinner, he put his hand on my shoulder as he passed my chair on his way to the living room, in a gesture of appropriate affection, which I treasured because I yearned for a good father. Appropriate touch, though, was uncommon.

I've often wondered why I trusted my father again one summer day in 1964 when I was twelve. I wanted to trust him, I needed to be able to trust him, and my year of innocent flirting with a male teacher, perhaps, suggested men could be trusted. He also didn't force me. He asked, "Do you want to go turtle hunting?" He was gathering gunnysacks and a harpoon, throwing them in the back of the '54 Ford truck. I was hoeing the green beans, sweat running down my forehead.

"Okay." Anything was better than slaving over the vegetables. I wiped my face with my dirty shirt. I leaned the hoe against the hundred-gallon gas tank we used to fill the farm machinery and got in the truck as my father opened the driver's door. I rolled down the window. He rolled up his sleeves, and patted my bare knee. His hand was rough and warm. Inside, I winced. But it had been several years since he'd last molested me, so I felt safe enough.

"Here, roll a cigarette for me," he said, handing me the Prince Albert can and motioning to the seat where the pack of thin cigarette papers lay. Threading the tobacco on the paper, I jostled it into a roll. I licked the paper, sealed the edge, and handed it to him. He lit it as I stared out the window. The aroma reminded me of the poker game my brothers had organized the previous Saturday night. Some older guys I didn't know sat at the dinner table, throwing cards and smoking. I had perched on a stool at the corner between two guys, watching. The cutest one, when smoke from a cigarette wafted my way, said, "Sorry, that smoke is getting in your pretty little eyes." No one had ever used that word to describe any part of me. I kept rolling "pretty" around in my mind as if it were a piece of Belgian chocolate melting on my tongue.

My father's voice interrupted my sweet daydream. "I heard about a bunch of big snappers in the creek across the section." He turned right at the corner a mile north.

Truthfully, I was a little scared of the ferocious turtles. The week before I'd seen one snap a broom handle in two when my father was showing Henry how dangerous they were. I'd heard how my father harpooned the animal's hard shells, but this was the first time I'd gone along to watch. Really, I just wanted to get out of the endless rows of beans.

I did like turtle meat, though, cooked in the pressure cooker until it wasn't so chewy. And turtle hearts, still beating after their bodies were torn apart, fascinated me. Like the chickens running headless around the barnyard after Mom's axe. Life didn't let go easily.

We didn't say much as we drove. When we got to the creek, my father stopped back a ways and grasped the harpoon, motioning me to bring a gunnysack. We picked our way through the tall grass at the edge of the cow pasture. A neighbor's steers were across the field, heads down, eating. I was glad of that. The big animals, though normally placid, still scared me.

"There!" Stopping, he flung his arm in front of me. His forearm brushed my emerging breasts. I jumped back.

"Don't move! You'll spook 'em!" He crept forward, keeping his eye on the biggest one as it rested in the sun. With a sharp crack, the harpoon penetrated the turtle's shell. He'd thrown it so fast I hadn't seen it leave his hand.

"Bring the sack." He pulled the prey out of the water, wrapped the sack around it, and snapped the harpoon out of the back. He walked back to the Ford and threw the sack in the back. I stood on the high bank at the edge of the creek enjoying the breeze and watching the other turtles that had returned to their sunny perches.

Before I realized it, my father had come up behind me. He'd thrown me down in the tall grass and begun fondling me. I couldn't believe it. I burst into tears.

"Oh, all right." he said, getting up and walking away.

I was too far away to walk home. I had to follow him. I ran to catch up with him, unsure whether he would leave me there if I wasn't at the truck when he was.

"I wouldn't have raped you." He stared straight ahead as I came alongside him.

I was silent. Rape? What was that? I'm not gonna ask him. And I was never, ever, going to be alone with him again. After a ride home in frozen silence, I ran to the safety of my room. Thankfully, he'd never molested me there. I reached for the dictionary to look up *rape*.

The two bright spots of my early life were school and sewing. At four, I sewed a pair of pants for Annie, my big walking doll. When my mother saw them, she said, "Making clothes for yourself is easier than sewing for dolls. I'll help you make a blouse." Together we cut out a Peter Pan–collared top. She sewed the seams on the black Necchi machine and I secured the collar facing and hem with wide hand stitches and proudly wore it to kindergarten.

Though food was plentiful on the farm, clothing was either second hand or homemade. At eleven years old, I began to sew my school wardrobe every August, tailoring my first wool suit just before my seventh grade year. The day I wore it for the first time, my teacher was so impressed, he asked me to show everyone. Feeding my heart on the attention, I twirled to the front of the class in my brown tweed skirt and jacket.

That teacher wasn't the only one who affirmed me. Several years earlier, in third grade, I had overheard my second-grade teacher say to my third-grade teacher: "Oh, yes, she's a good worker!" I beamed as they smiled my direction. In addition to Mr. Edwards in sixth grade, three of my seventh and eighth grade teachers were male, all of whom spoke to me with interest and respect. In high school, Mr. Brown sometimes put his arm around my waist as we walked down the hall. I was starved for safe male touch. And in the company of those teachers, I felt safe, smart, and valued. My parents, however, disdained teachers. They often said: "Those who can, do; those who can't, teach." But it was teachers who reflected back to me a positive image of myself. Their view of me gave me a future.

By my freshman year, I began to dream of that future. My brothers had all gone into the military soon after high school. My sister had married after beauty school, settling down a few miles away. Encouraged by my teachers, I planned to go to college, first the regional junior college, then one of the public four-year schools in Illinois. My grades would secure tuition assistance, and I could work for room and board. Not that I had much vision of a new life—just the certainty that I had to escape my father. Like most sexual abuse victims, I had little sense of a future. A void loomed beyond college.

Social unease increased my desire to leave town. I felt as out of place in high school as an eight-year-old would feel at a White House dinner. No one wanted me to sit with them, the conversation confused me, and my homemade clothes marked me as an outsider.

One awful night, my inadequacy was exposed at a dance after a basketball game. In semidarkness, on the stage of the school gym, the local longhairs struck the first notes of "Louie, Louie." The platform glittered with the revolving colored lights the band had set up to reflect off their shiny electric guitars. The rock n' roll rhythms of the sock hop reverberated around the small space. I'd walked onto the dance floor to talk to Diane, a classmate who rode the bus with me. She'd introduced me to Gary, whom I knew as one of the cutest guys in the area, but had never met him. I'd stammered a greeting and had been listening to their banter in the interval between songs.

When the music began again, Diane turned to me. "You dance with Gary." I froze as she walked away. Diane wasn't exactly a friend, but sometimes we discussed homework assignments on the long bus ride. That afternoon, she had asked if I was going to the dance after the basketball game that evening, and I impulsively had said, "Yes."

"I'll see you there." She had said, as she ran down the bus steps. I'd watched as she hurried across the gravel road. What had I just said? If I don't go, she'll tease me the rest of the year. I rarely went to the dances, though I often went to the basketball games, usually sitting alone, but enjoying the fast action and the feeling of crowd solidarity as we cheered on the varsity Panthers. Normally, I bypassed the music spilling out of the open door of the gym where the sock hops were held. Nobody saw me cry myself to sleep those nights.

Tonight, I'd been sitting on the sidelines, enjoying the music, knowing I'd die of embarrassment if I tried to make my body move like everybody else. I'd never look like them, coordinated, graceful. If I were watching *American Bandstand* with Dick Clark, I'd have given "Louie, Louie" an 85, a good beat, easy to dance to. But I wasn't in my living room, alone on a Saturday morning, with the glass boundary between the dancers and me, trying to imitate their smooth movements.

When Diane left me, I was right in the middle of wiggling bodies, in a dark room, rooted to the floor, close enough to this blonde god that I could smell his Brut cologne over the residue of sweat in the gym mingled with the aroma of teenage hormones.

"Let's dance," Gary said. He took my arm.

I glanced up at his smile, but not even his kind eyes gave me enough courage. "I just can't!" Jerking free, I ran, picking my way through pulsing waves of dancers intent on melding to the music. On the way out, I bumped Diane, dancing with a new boy. She stared at me.

"I can't do it. I can't dance!" I kept moving, averting my eyes, until I reached the open door, though I thought Mr. Brown, one of the chaperones, threw me a smile as I rushed by.

Did you have to embarrass yourself like that? Couldn't you have just stood there and swayed? Everybody else can dance; what's wrong with you? I ran to the car and sped home. Gasping for breath, I threw myself on my bed and finally cried myself to sleep. Added to the secret shame of the abuse, this latest shame nearly choked me.

I pinned most of my hope of deliverance from this wilderness on attracting a man. Men got the goodies and made the rules. I saw my mother serve my father his dinner, no matter how tired she was. I experienced his arbitrary power over my body. "It's a man's world" was an accepted maxim. As far as I was concerned, however, I had missed my one chance when I ran out of the dance. I'd have despaired but for two angels Father-God sent. Not that I recognized his provision until years later.

In the fall of my sophomore year, several 4-H clubs jointly offered a bus trip to Chicago to tour a pretzel factory and go to the Schubert Theatre to see *Hello Dolly*. 4-H is a social and educational group, like a coed Scout club, encompassing kids from several schools. I almost didn't get to go. As my mother was driving me into town, she reported that my father had balked at letting me go when he realized I was the only one from Halesburg going. In a rare moment of self-assertion, she'd gone to bat for me against my father's distrust of outsiders.

Having little contact with boys beyond Halesburg, I was excited. I made a new dress, of a yellow and dark red paisley print, falling from an empire waist with a deep inverted pleat down the front. Unlike my usual sense of bare adequacy, that day I felt elegant and stylish. Just as I'd hoped, though it was beyond my wildest dreams, a young man, George, noticed.

After the factory tour and lunch at a cafeteria, we roamed the downtown streets together. Small-town kids in the big city, we looked wide-eyed at the elegant windows, holding hands in a flush of first love. When we got to the theatre, we were chagrined to realize our seats were many rows apart. But my seat was next to an empty single.

"Maybe, when this person comes, I can ask him to switch with you!" I could hardly believe I was saying that. I didn't talk to strangers. But I had to take the chance, this time. When the missing man showed up and with an understanding smile said, "Oh, sure, I'd be happy to," I floated up the steps of the darkened theatre to tell George to come take his seat next to me. Though little came of this relationship, God planted a seed of hope.

Even more hopeful was the kindness of a young relative of my sister's husband. Rick also treated me with interest and respect on the occasional times when I saw him at my sister's house. One night we sat out on the back steps, talking into the night. What we said wasn't important. That he spent the time with me sent the message that I was likeable. When junior prom time came, I called him.

In spite of living an hour away, he said, yes, he would take me to prom and post prom and the picnic the next day. I made a chiffon dress for the formal dance and a flowered short set for the post-prom

CHAPTER 5

PARENTING MYSELF

omebody was asking for you yesterday. Asked about that girl with the great smile." The other car hop threw the last phrase over her shoulder as she passed me, juggling a tray with four glass mugs of root beer. It was the summer before college, and I was an outdoor waitress at the A&W.

"Really? What kind of car did he drive?" I turned, with a customer's order in hand, and followed her.

Attaching the tray to the half-rolled up window of her customer, she said, "I dunno. Something green. That'll be $2.15, please," she said to her customer.

My boss stuck his head out the window. "Karen!" He must have seen the white paper in my hand.

"Coming!" I scurried to the window, my heart fluttering. Since the short relationship with George from the 4-H trip and another short-lived connection, no boy had shown any interest in me. Handing in the order, I thought, I bet it's the guy who gave me a quarter tip last week. Usually our tips were nickels and dimes. Leaning against the ledge, I didn't see the new customer pull up at the end of the row of cars until the other carhop broke my reverie. "That one's yours!"

I started down the row of parked cars. Oh, my goodness, it's him. Blonde hair above a chiseled face, arm hanging out the window, cigarette in his mouth, in a green Buick Skylark.

"Hey, I asked about you yesterday. I'm Roger." He grinned at me, flicking the ash off his cigarette into the car's ashtray. He smoked the same unfiltered Camels as that long-ago poker player who'd said I had "pretty eyes."

"So I heard. I'm Karen." My palms sweated as I smiled. I couldn't think what else to say as this blonde man stared.

"How about a date? Saturday?" He shielded his eyes with his left hand as he looked up at me.

"Uh, sure!" I floated through the rest of my shift. Maybe my dreams of a new life after high school were coming true.

When he pulled into the farmyard at 7:00 on Saturday evening, I was watching at the window, dressed in the flowered cotton outfit I'd worn to post-prom. After I introduced him to my parents, we set off. I sat next to him on the bench seat, my heart thumping. I tried to remember all the dating advice I'd devoured in *Seventeen* magazine.

He lit a cigarette. "Let's just go for a drive, okay?"

"Sure, that's fine." We pulled out of the gravel driveway toward town. *Seventeen* said to be agreeable. They also advised to get him to talk about himself. "So, what do you do?"

"I pack paper cups into cartons at a factory. I graduated from high school two years ago." When we'd chatted briefly at the A&W, I'd learned he was from Plano, which was on Route 34, closer to Chicago. He laid his elbow along the closed window, holding the cigarette.

"Do you like it?"

"It's a living. My dad works there; he got me the job." He took a puff, exhaling a smoke ring.

"I'm going to college in the fall." The smoke hung in the enclosed air.

"You must really like school. I didn't like it much." He tapped the ash into the ashtray.

"Did you like any classes?"

"No, not really." We pulled to a stop at Route 34. "East or West?"

"West." My heart slowed. My family took Sunday afternoon drives like that, each of us taking turns setting direction at the intersections. Roger and I continued in that manner, changing the subject away from our obvious differences. At 10:00, we approached La Salle. He soon pulled into a Pizza Hut and stubbed out his cigarette.

"Hungry?"

"A little." He opened the door and I scooted out on the driver's side into the fresh air. He led me inside. I grinned at him as we sat down, after he'd slotted a quarter into the jukebox. The quirky rhythms of "Magic Carpet Ride" livened up the traditional décor of red and white checked tablecloths covering small square tables.

"This is nice." I'd rarely been inside any restaurant, and I'd never been inside a Pizza Hut before. The dark wood created a cozy atmosphere. My mouth watered at the cheesy tomato smell.

When we arrived back at the farmyard at midnight, he leaned over and kissed me. I'd never been kissed. As he held my lips, a shot of arousal warmed me. I pulled away.

"I'd better get in." The arousal had shaken me.

"When can I see you again?"

"I'm off Thursday."

"Thursday it is, then."

As I sank into sleep that night, I replayed the kiss in my mind, savoring the pleasure of it. In the dry wilderness of my heart, sexual arousal felt like sustenance.

As we continued seeing each other, heavy petting ended every date. His obvious desire for me watered my thirsty heart.

In the fall, I moved to Oglesby to attend Illinois Valley Community College (IVCC). In high school, I'd made one friend, Jane, whom I'd met in Catholic Youth Organization meetings. Along with her friend, Mary, we took an apartment in a building being renovated from offices to apartments. Under twelve-foot ceilings, we occupied a tiny kitchen, a small living room, an enormous bedroom, a tiny bath, and an additional room beyond the bedroom that functioned as a closet for the three of us.

Together, we ate grilled cheese sandwiches and cabbage salad, rode the bus to the college, and began our new life. I walked to mass every Sunday. Roger and I continued our relationship. Every Saturday night, we ate Pizza Hut pizza, listened to "Magic Carpet Ride," and made out in his Buick, or on my couch if my roommates weren't home. Since good Catholic girls didn't use birth control and I was terrified of pregnancy, I refused intercourse. Within a few months, though, the routine bored me, especially as I met new college boys. A more exciting future beckoned.

When Roger picked me up for Christmas break, I threw my bag in the back and plopped in the front passenger side seat. I stared out the windshield.

"This relationship isn't going to work."

"What do you mean? What do you want?" He laid his hand on my shoulder. "I love you. I'll do anything."

I stiffened. "I know. But it's just over, okay? I'm sorry."

We drove to the farm in silence. I didn't have words to explain that I had to get out of Halesburg. He'd stayed in his little town. I couldn't. I didn't know where I was going, but I had begun to hope I was going somewhere. With someone who liked more than one song at one restaurant.

I returned to Oglesby after Christmas break. Through an oral interpretation class, I'd gotten involved in the junior college performing arts community. Though my talent was small, the group of theatre people let me hang out with them. At lunch, we took over a room off the student lounge, which served as the gathering spot on campus. For the first time, during daily lunch hours and long evenings of play rehearsal, I connected with a group.

In a reader's theatre performance that spring, I read a solo piece of a young woman waiting for a telephone call. For fifteen minutes, I begged, cajoled, and threatened destruction to that black instrument to try to make it ring. No one needed to coach me. I'd been waiting for a telephone to ring since I was four years old. Someone who would call for me. Someone who would rescue me from my loneliness and fear.

In the sexual activity with Roger, I'd discovered the power of arousal to blunt that loneliness. After breaking up with Roger, I was readily sexual, short of intercourse, with almost any man who glanced my way. In the half-renovated office building where we lived, I'd often greeted a good-looking, sweaters and chinos guy. He lived upstairs. Feeling lonely one night, I knocked on his door.

"Hi. I don't think I've introduced myself. I'm Karen." I smiled as he opened the door.

"I'm Jack. Wanna come in?" He swept the door wide open and stepped aside. The space consisted of one office-sized room with a corner kitchenette. The brown sofa-bed was upright, the pillow and white sheets folded on one end. *Laugh-In* was on TV. A desk lamp in the corner was the only other illumination.

He sat down and patted the couch. "Watch TV with me?"

"Sure." I sat next to him. On the screen, Goldie Hawn was dancing in a flowered bikini.

Jack draped his arm behind my shoulders. When he started touching me, I relaxed into his arms. When the phone rang, he jumped up.

"Oh, not much. Just watching *Laugh-In*. What are you doing?" He turned his back to me.

"I'm thinking about you, too, Sweetie."

Sweetie?

"I'm meeting the photographer Saturday. I've seen his work. He's good."

My stomach turned sour as I listened to his end of the conversation.

"Yeah, I can't wait either, Honey."

"Okay, see you Sunday at your mom's. I'll bring the information about the photographer."

"Love you, too. Bye." He replaced the phone in its cradle and turned back to me. Smiling, he sat down and put his arm around me.

"Who was that?"

"Joyce."

"Who's that?"

"Uh, my fiancée."

I jumped up. "Fiancée! You didn't tell me you were engaged."

"Why does that matter? This is just for fun. She'll never know." He pulled me down onto his lap.

I struggled out of his grasp. "I'd better be going. See you around." I closed the door behind me.

In those days, my approach to men was informed by a combination of Catholic morality and using them for pleasure. Though some glimmers of hope for the future were rising, a constant dull ache resided behind my breastbone. Only sexual arousal blunted that pain. But there were limits to my sexual activity. I would not encourage a man to cheat on his fiancée.

On my terms, however, there were few limits to my willingness to use a man. I must have developed a reputation as a tease among the theatre group, as I was sexual with anyone who showed any interest. Our encounters lasted only long enough to satisfy me, though. Their needs were immaterial. One guy quite seriously sat me down and explained the physical consequences for a man if a sexual experience is begun but not finished. But I didn't care if my pleasure came at their pain. Without recognizing it, I was replaying the abuse scenario, giving myself the powerful place.

But I met my match in the Vietnam veteran that I fell for in the spring. Ed was even more self-absorbed than I was. I first noticed him when he spoke on campus after the Kent State incident. National Guardsmen had killed four unarmed war protestors, and campus rallies were held around the country to register outrage. Ed, in green fatigues and army-issue sunglasses, spoke from a platform erected in the courtyard in front of the student union.

"Now they're killing us. The military-industrial complex isn't satisfied just to kill the Vietcong. We could be next. Nobody's safe anymore."

I stared at him as he continued his speech. Was it possible my government might kill me? When the rally ended, he approached me. "You're looking pretty serious, little lady." His dark eyes twinkled as he pushed back his silky blonde hair.

"Well, I should think so. This is serious stuff." I matched his light tone.

"Oh well, we can't really do anything about it anyway." He threw his hands in the air.

"Were you there? In 'Nam?"

"Yeah, I was a grunt." He grimaced, glancing away.

"What are you doing now?"

"Just messing around. Want to mess around with me?"

"Sure." Over the next few weeks, we developed a highly sexualized relationship, but I still stopped short of intercourse.

At semester's end, the night before returning to the farm, Ed came over. Jane and Mary had already left. My mother was picking me up in the morning.

We were sitting on the shabby couch furnished with the apartment when a tear rolled down my face.

"Hey, don't cry. I'll come up to Halesburg to see you." He tightened his arm around me and pulled up my face for a kiss. "Let me make love to you. I won't see you for a while."

I squirmed out of his grasp. "No, it's not a good time of the month."

"Okay. But, you know, someday you'll say 'yes.'"

His dark eyes drew me in as he held my gaze.

In the first part of the summer, I was too excited to miss Ed. Midyear, I'd earned membership in Phi Theta

Kappa, the national junior college honor society. In the spring, I had played Mrs. Webb in a reader's theatre presentation of *Our Town* that we entered in their national convention. We won first place. That meant free tuition to a ten-day Drama Institute in upstate New York. Ellen, who'd played Emily Gibbs, met me at O'Hare. My brothers, all in the military, had at various times flown from O'Hare. But flying was new to me. In fact, I'd never been farther away from home than Wisconsin.

I said goodbye to my mother at the gate and floated down the jetway. Ellen had gone to buy a paperback. Finding my window seat, I leaned back. I could hardly believe I got to go. New York City! Flying! Broadway! I smiled at myself in the reflection in the window. I could smell the musky perfume of the blonde woman settling into the seat ahead of me. Ellen sat down beside me and stashed her makeup case under the seat in front of her.

"Have you flown before?" I asked. She looked like she belonged in the jet set in her sleek hair and polished nails. As usual, I felt like a country bumpkin with my bitten nails and flyaway hair.

"Oh yeah, lots of times." She picked up her paperback.

I stared out the window as we began to move. I shouldn't be so excited. It's not that big a deal. I pulled at a loose cuticle.

We landed at Kennedy and found the shuttle toward Grand Central Terminal to catch the train to Poughkeepsie. I followed Ellen into the bus, watching what she did with her suitcase. With my bag stowed, I crowded ahead of her. "Let me have the window seat," I said.

"Sure, it's your first time," she said.

The city skyline looked like a postcard as we sped along the Long Island Freeway. As we emerged from the Mid-Town Tunnel, the Empire State building looked like a photo from a textbook. Ellen read her paperback. I picked up the *Glamour* magazine I'd brought with me. New York City didn't look any different than its photos.

At Grand Central, Ellen said, "It's two hours until the train leaves. Let's have a drink."

"What's the legal age in New York?" I gathered the drinking age differed from state to state.

"Oh, it's eighteen here." She led the way into a walnut-paneled restaurant. She ordered wine. I ordered Coke. My drinking days were still ahead of me.

The Institute at Bennett College was devoted to studying drama, including two days in New York City seeing plays, and meeting industry insiders like the New York Times theatre critic Clive Barnes. I, however, was more interested in the guys. I quickly hooked up with Joe, a young man from New Jersey.

The second night, we hung out all night, wandering around the grounds, kissing and making out. He was from Newark. I basked in the glow of his sophistication. In the morning we were supposed to spend the day in Stratford, Connecticut, attending a dress rehearsal of *As You Like It*.

"Oh, I don't want to go. I don't like Shakespeare. Stay with me," he said. We were walking back to the dorms after breakfast. Though I'd been awake all night, I didn't feel sleepy.

"Okay. Let's walk into town." We spent the day poking around the nearby village.

But I had second thoughts by the time I went to bed that night in the room I shared with Ellen. She blew in at 11 P.M., her eyes shiny, her brown hair flying.

"Didn't you go today?" She said when she saw me in bed.

"No, I hung out here. Was it good?"

"Was it good?! It was Shakespeare!"

As she told me about the play, I thought, you dummy. You should've gone. Why let a guy determine your day?

The next morning, heading to the breakfast line, I glanced around the cafeteria. I didn't see Joe.

The guy ahead of me in line smiled. "Hi." His face was pockmarked, but his eyes were steady and calm.

"Hi. The food is pretty good here, don't you think?"

"Beats cooking for myself, that's for sure. I'm Neil." He picked up a tray, and helped himself to some scrambled eggs and toast.

"I'm Karen. Nice to meet you." I picked up a single serving box of Wheaties and a banana. We carried our trays to an empty table.

"So, how did you like yesterday?" Neil asked as he dug into his food.

"I didn't go." I said, peeling my banana.

"You didn't go! Why not?" He stopped chewing his toast and raised his eyebrows.

"I didn't feel like it. I'm a dummy." I couldn't meet his eyes. I took a gulp of water.

"It's okay. We're all dummies." He reached over his water glass and patted my hand, still grasping my glass.

We went to our classes together that day, chatting and laughing together. He was from Texas, and this was his first trip out of state, too. His excitement rekindled mine.

After dinner we went back to his room. I sat in the desk chair while he sprawled on the bed. He'd snuck in a six-pack. After his sixth beer, he looked at the window and said, "I'm going to jump out that window!"

"Neil! Why are you going to do that?" I laughed, not believing him.

He staggered to the open window and glanced into the darkness. "Just to say I did."

I reached for him, but he was gone before I touched him. I ran out of the room, down the stairs, and rushed out to the side of the building, where Neil lay on the grass moaning, holding his ankle.

"Neil, are you okay?" I looked up at the window. The windows in the front of the grand mansion were five feet off the ground. But it was built into a hill. Here in the back, in the dorm rooms, they were fifteen feet up.

"Yikes! I thought it was only a five-foot drop, like the front."

"Never mind. You need ice on that ankle. Can you stand up?" I helped him to his feet and offered him my shoulder. Together we hobbled to the elevator.

"Man, that's the dumbest thing I've ever done." He winced as the elevator shook when it stopped at the second floor.

"You weren't thinking, Neil. You just assumed this window was like the front ones. We're all dummies, remember?" He leaned on me as he limped to his bed.

"Well, yeah. But the elevator at the end of the hall should have been a clue it was higher!" He rubbed his ankle.

"Yes. Just stop. I'll get some ice. You just made a mistake. Everybody makes mistakes." I opened the door to look for an ice machine.

With Neil, I noticed something new in myself. Empathy. At the time, I didn't really know where it came from. But he'd been kind to me. And winning the trip to the Institute for elite college students fed my self-worth. Out of that enhanced self-regard, I could give comfort. I could bear not only my own burden of shame, but also help Neil bear his. Rather than add to his embarrassment by laughing at him, I could relieve some of it with understanding. He felt so grateful to me that when we went into the city on Wednesday, he took me to the famous Sardi's restaurant.

CHAPTER 6

LOST IN THE WILDERNESS

Back in Halesburg, the momentary vitality I'd felt in New York soon died. The rest of my summer consisted of emptying bedpans for my ailing grandmother and waiting for Ed to visit. Thankfully, after flying helicopters in Vietnam, my brother Craig was home for the summer. We spent a lot of evenings in his MG convertible, the wind flying through our hair. Other than at meals, I avoided my parents. Suppertime was a command performance full of trivial conversation.

I never heard from Ed, and when I returned to Oglesby in the fall he was with someone else. Ignoring my feelings of rejection, I looked for someone else, too. Mary and Jane didn't return to school, so I found a couple of college freshman girls from Halesburg who had space for a roommate. Down the road from the renovated office building, I moved into an upstairs three-bedroom apartment with Jill and Lynn. I spray-painted an old refrigerator avocado green. I found a utility wire spool to use for a kitchen table. Our chairs were milk can stools, also painted avocado. But I didn't really know my new roommates, and we didn't get along well.

Jill had been elected to the homecoming court twice in high school. The dance I ran out of and the junior prom were the only two Halesburg dances I'd attended. Not only were Jill and Lynn good friends, but four more of their friends lived in the back apartment in our building. In a hall closet, there was a door between the apartments, which they used freely.

Alone, I often wandered the streets of Oglesby, pondering the meaning of life. Mass began to feel meaningless, so I stopped going. The rituals meant nothing to me. They only reminded me of a childhood I'd just as soon forget. "Truth" mattered to me but, I concluded, God was unknowable.

One October night, I wandered past one of many corner taverns in the small town. Early in the semester, I'd found a couple of male drinking buddies. I wasn't sexual with either of them. Drinking, which they paid for, had become a new way to blunt the pain.

The dark bar pulled me in. Opening the door, I inhaled the now familiar smell of whiskey and beer. At a small table past the wooden bar, my English professor from last year was seated, alone. Unlike his usual frown, he looked pensive and vulnerable. I had worked on the literary magazine with him last year, and he'd even published a poem I'd written about my relationship with Roger, saying it was "pretty good." High praise, coming from him.

"Hey, Mr. Leonard, can I join you?" My stomach fluttered. Though I stammered next to his erudition, I liked to discuss philosophy with him. Without the anchor of Catholicism, I was adrift. I especially liked to talk about existentialism, which he embraced. It made sense to me. Anxiety, nothingness, meaning-lessness: that's exactly what life was.

He motioned to the opposite chair.

"What'll you have?" He took a drag on his Marlboro.

"Seven-seven, if you're buying, thanks." I'd learned to like the whiskey and 7UP combination.

He returned to the table with the drink. "Enjoying the evening?" He took a sip of his Manhattan.

"As much as I enjoy anything these days. If everything is meaningless, how do you live?"

His face was momentarily obscured as he blew out smoke. "You make your own meaning." He waved the smoke away, giving me a grave look.

"How do you make meaning? I don't even make my bed." Then I felt silly. Those things weren't even in the same category. It just came out.

But he smiled before he spoke. "It's a leap of faith, Karen. That's all it is. You just make a choice."

"I decide that life is meaningful." My tone was flat.

"Right."

"I don't know if I can do that or not. I'll think about it. Thanks for the drink. I'll see you Monday."

This was too much. If my life had no meaning, what if I couldn't make one up? Nothing justified my existence. I was useless, and nobody loved me. My mind churned as I returned to the street.

I wandered to the far end of Walnut Street. A man in a blue Pontiac pulled up alongside me.

"Hey, want a ride?" I leaned down to check him out. He looked clean.

"Sure." Not that I was going anywhere. I opened the door and slid onto the bench seat, staying on my side.

"What are you up to tonight?" He pulled away from the curb, heading west.

"Not much. You?"

"I'm driving around looking for cute chicks to pick up. Looks like I found one."

"Looks like." I rolled down the window and let the fresh air blow over me.

We drove around Oglesby for a while, talking about nothing. He must have taken my measure by then because he drove out into the country and he stopped by the side of the road. He took my arm, pulled me close, and kissed me.

"Hey, don't do that." I pushed off him. I may have been loose with guys I knew, but this stranger was different.

"So, whaddya get in the car for, then?"

I could not explain my lostness.

He sneered at me, but didn't pursue it. Starting the car, he squealed his tires as he pulled away, hightailing it back to the downtown street where he let me out.

You'd think that would have scared me. I barely thought about it, though I didn't get into any other strangers' cars. I did, however, fall in with Chuck and Dave, who were heroin addicts. I didn't know they were users when I first met them through the local girl who worked at the grocery store and lived in the next block. I'd begun hanging out with her and her friends on the weekends, when I wasn't running around town with my drinking buddies.

One November day, when I was walking the streets on a Saturday afternoon, Chuck and Dave, along with a couple of buddies, pulled up to the curb beside me.

"Hey, wanna get in? We've got some good horse."
I vaguely thought *horse* meant some kind of drug,
but these guys were buddies. They were okay. I
wouldn't do drugs with them, but I was grateful for
the company.

"Sure." I climbed in the back of the old two-door
Cadillac as Dave, in the passenger seat, leaned
forward to let me in. "What are you guys doing?"

Chuck, driving, looked at me in the mirror.
"We're floating, man. This is the best we've ever
gotten." He glanced back at the road, just in time
to swerve away from an orange construction cone
blocking the lane where the concrete had been cut
out, leaving a twelve-inch drop off. "Oh, man."

Dave said, "Yeah, man, we'd a gotten stuck in
the hole, man." He laughed, taking a drag on his
cigarette and tipping his beer can into his mouth,
spilling half the swallow down the front of his
already dirty shirt. The beer smell added another
layer to the smells left by years of legal and illegal
substances consumed in this once luxury car.

"Hey, I gotta pee." The guy on my left began to
hold his crotch.

"We'll go out to the house." The driver sped up.
I was trapped between the two guys in the back,
hoping he could hold it and that we'd get there in
one piece.

"House" was a figurative word. With these guys, I had previously roamed Oglesby's network of shadowy back roads populated with shacks, but I had not been to one of their places. Pulling off the main road onto one of these dirt paths, we pulled up to a square building with peeling paint, sporting a garage door half off its tracks and a regular door standing open. Inside the door, a stairway rose to the second floor, without a railing. The first floor was full of scraps of gray lumber, sodden drywall, and assorted pieces of trash I couldn't identify.

The second floor came into view as I ascended the stairs. In the corner stood a small stove, encrusted with grease. Next to it, on a stack of pallets, was an apartment-sized refrigerator. The end tables were upended orange crates. It didn't look like they used the stove much, unless they heated food in the cans. Sometime in the last three weeks they'd eaten baked beans. The half-empty cans were now languishing on the crates, spoons stuck in them, covered with green mold.

What am I doing here? Where am I going?

The crotch-holder did his business and we tramped down the stairs. As we pulled out of the driveway I stared at the broken garage door. "I gotta go home."

"Oh man, really? Are you sure?" Chuck glanced at me in the rear view mirror.

"We're going out to Starved Rock," Dave said. "Come with us."

"No, I need to go home." Suddenly I knew I didn't want to go anywhere these guys were going.

They let me out on the sidewalk in front of the apartment, where I ran up the stairs without saying goodbye. Going into my bedroom, I closed the door and sprawled on the unmade bed. The wind outside blew through the loose windows, ruffling the brown and gold geometric patterned curtains I'd made from fabric my mother had bought for me. Wrapping myself in the matching comforter, I bawled as if my tears were inexhaustible.

Nobody would ever love me. I dug my fingers into my pillows and wiped my soggy nose in sheets stiff with previous snot. My head throbbed. I gulped air through my mouth. As my sinuses filled up with congestion, my soul emptied. Why am I even alive? What is the point? If my roommates were home, they didn't check on me. How had I arrived at the backside of this desert, where people ate beans out of cans and left them where they lay until the mold grew?

I thought about Charlie, a fellow student I had dated a couple of times. We'd stayed friends after our brief romance. Last week, he confessed his despair over ever finding someone who would love him. "Short, big nose, freckles, not that smart or I'd be at a four-year college—who's going to want me? Sometimes I think I should just end it all, but I would hate to leave somebody with the mess to clean up."

"I don't care about that. I just don't wanna suffer," I'd said.

Charlie! He's picking me up for dress rehearsal in ten minutes! I was Rebecca Gibbs, the sister of the male lead, in *Our Town*. Charlie's part was even smaller.

I jumped up, washed my face, and gathered my costume just in time to hear his car horn.

He glanced at my red face as I threw my little-girl dress in the back seat. "What's the matter?" A tear rolled down my cheek.

As he drove, I told him about the pigsty I'd found myself in. I leaned my elbow on the window, holding my forehead in my hand, not looking at him. My best buddies were alcoholics, my drive-around buddies were heroin addicts, and what did that make me? "Some days, I just want to die." I stared at my feet.

He glanced at me as we crossed the Illinois River. "I know. I know what you mean. But what if it didn't work? Then what—we'd be vegetables? Life's gotta get better. That's all I have to say." He clicked the radio on.

"It better." I managed to smile at him. I knew Charlie understood. I took a deep breath and consciously relaxed my shoulders.

We gossiped about the other cast members, and then sang along with "Everything is Beautiful." Beautiful? I wasn't even pretty, and my life was nowhere near beautiful. But the kindness in Charlie's eyes took the edge off my mood. When we got to the old theatre where we rehearsed, I changed into my costume. In pigtails and a brown gingham dress with a big brown bow at the neck, I looked twelve. After my first act scene was finished, I plopped down in a seat to watch the rest of the familiar story.

In the third act, the female lead, Emily, dies. Then, in a deal with the Stage Manager, she gets to step back in time to her twelfth birthday. She sweeps around the stage, exalting in life's poignancy of "new-ironed dresses and hot baths." After this epiphany, she speaks to the Stage Manager. "Do any human beings ever realize life while they live it—every, every minute?"

He shook his head. "No—saints and poets maybe—they do some."[1]

Emily sank into her seat among the dead.

I wiped away a tear.

When the lights came up after rehearsal, I wandered out front. Entering the half-dark lobby, I recognized a young man from last year's apartment building. He stood before the house light switches in the electrical panel. He was older, at least twenty-five, tall, with shoulder-length brown hair and a beard. Last year, I had said "Hi" when he passed me on the stairs one night, but he'd walked by like I wasn't there.

I bounced up to him now. "Hi, remember me?" I smiled big, pigtails flopping around my head.

"No." But he did answer, and he half-smiled. I didn't need much encouragement.

"I lived downstairs from you last year." I twiddled my pigtail. "I'm Karen."

"I'm Jerry Rabbitt. What are you doing here?" He glanced into the auditorium, where we could hear the sounds of the stage crew cleaning up.

"I'm Rebecca, can't you tell? I don't dress like this everyday." I shrugged my shoulders and lifted my hands.

"Well, you must be older than you look." We bantered back and forth for a few more minutes until the director called for all the cast to assemble to hear his final performance notes.

After getting Jerry's attention on top of Charlie's kindness, I felt stronger, and my suicidal thoughts from earlier in the day receded. Suicide was a vague idea that I carried around like a security blanket. If life got too bad, killing myself was an escape. But I never even considered how I'd do it, much less made a specific plan. I was too afraid of going to hell. And after meeting Jerry that day, my love life picked up. But not with him—at least, not at first.

Soon after *Our Town*, I met Eddie in sociology class and got involved with him. He was a fair-haired artist with a winsome way about him. Now, I realize, I didn't feel worthy of him. I hung out with drug addicts; he was a church-going Presbyterian. I was wandering; he was focused on his painting. He was a virgin. I seduced him. Using condoms, I finally went all the way to intercourse. We began dating in the spring of 1971, and, after a few months, because of my deep sense of unworthiness, I quite unconsciously sabotaged that relationship. Ed, the Vietnam vet I had been with the previous spring, reentered my life. One night when Eddie was away, I found myself in bed with Ed. Ed was right. I did say "yes." Or shall I say, I couldn't say "no." Then I felt compelled to "confess" that indiscretion to Eddie. He was furious and that was the end of that. I was a worm. What a jerk I was.

I went to the Phi Theta Kappa national convention again in the spring and hooked up with a couple of guys, unlike the previous summer when I'd been able to maintain good sexual boundaries with Neil at the Institute.

When summer came, I stayed in Oglesby to take classes and work on campus, unwilling to be at the farm with my parents. One June day, after my work of checking papers for the English department head, Dr. Whalen, I was studying in the theatre room at one end of the nearly deserted student center. Through the glass wall that separated that room from the main lounge, I noticed Jerry enter the far door, heading for the vending machines in the enclosed room on the other side of the building.

We'd greeted each other around campus that spring semester after our brief encounter at the *Our Town* rehearsal, but nothing had developed between us. I jumped up and trotted the length of the brown paneled lounge. I entered the vending machine area from the other side. "Hey, how ya doing?"

"Oh, hi, Karen." He glanced up at me as he inserted coins into a machine. "Want a chocolate chip cookie?"

"Sure." He'd never even bought me a Coke before. My part-time student work was my only income. A cookie was a treat.

He handed me the cookie, and we walked back to the empty theatre room, where the performers usually gathered around the institutional tables. In a corner of the room, a group of gray upholstered chairs formed an informal seating area. We took seats across from each other.

He smiled. "What are you up to?" The fluorescents flickered overhead. One of the ballasts was humming.

"Just studying. You?" I took a bite of the cookie and crumbs spilled down the front of my blue knit top.

"I'm taking a pottery class. This is break time." Pointing at my shirt, he said, "You're sure spilling crumbs."

"Yeah, I'm pretty good at crumb-sprinkling." I grinned.

"Crumb-sprinkling, huh." Grinning back at me, he bit off his own cookie.

"Yeah, crumb-sprinkling. It's fun. You should try it." I took another bite, making more crumbs.

"With you, maybe." He crumbled half his remaining cookie down the front of his shirt. "I'll bet you know how to crumb-sprinkle really good." He laughed.

"Why, yes, Mr. Rabbitt, I do. Maybe you'd like to find out sometime." I was nothing if not forward.

"Well, we'll have to see about that. Want a ride home?" He finished the rest of his cookie and brushed the crumbs off his shirt into a wastebasket.

"I have my bike."

"That's okay. It'll fit in my Mustang."

"Cool."

We began to date then, as he often skipped out on the second hour of his pottery class to take me home. On our first formal date we ate at a supper club. He had to tell me which fork to use when. My lack of social knowledge didn't seem to bother Jerry, though, as we spent more and more time together. We were both more suited to the outdoors than fine dining, so we enjoyed hiking the deep canyons at Starved Rock and Matthiessen State Park and riding around in the blue Mustang he'd bought when he was in the navy in Norfolk. He had gone into the navy rather than being drafted into the army. He had been able to observe the war from off the coast of Da Nang rather than trudging through the jungles of Vietnam. Now he was attending college on the GI Bill, which provided tuition and a stipend for room and board. He lived in the top floor of an old house in La Salle. Painting for his landlord supplemented his income.

Compared to the previous summer of emptying bedpans on the farm, this summer was shaping up nicely. But I nearly sabotaged our growing relationship, just as I had destroyed the relationship with Eddie. Jerry and I were crossing the bridge into La Salle one evening on our way to the drive-in movie. I faced him in the car, a half-smile on my face. "I'm really a prostitute and a drug addict, you know." I didn't think about it; the words just came out.

"What?" He stared straight ahead, his fingers gripping the wheel.

"Yeah, I turn tricks and shoot up horse." I was just messing with him, of course. I was almost a virgin, or so I liked to tell myself, and I had never touched heroin.

His eyes reddened as he stared straight ahead. "Everything I touch turns to dirt."

"Oh, no, I'm just kidding." I was horrified at his pain.

He glanced at me, eyebrows raised, a tear slipping down his cheek. "Kidding?" He shook his head.

"Didn't you see my smile?" As we drove through town toward the theatre, I apologized repeatedly.

"Just forget it, okay?" We'd joined the line of cars at the entrance by then, and we said no more, losing ourselves in *MASH*. We'd seen it before, but we laughed at all the same places: Hawkeye's antics, the "pros from Dover," and the shower scene with Hot Lips. But we missed a lot of it, making out in the back seat.

My cruelty was a grown-up version of spanking my little first grade classmates. I was the perpetrator, the powerful one. But this time, I did it for real and saw the pain I had caused. I took no pleasure in it. I didn't know why I needed to be the powerful one. I just did what I felt like, and, that day, cruelty was it. But seeing his pain cured me. I was never so nasty again.

We continued seeing each other that summer of 1971, even though I was moving a hundred miles south to attend the University of Illinois in Urbana-Champaign that fall. Jerry was just a summer fling.

CHAPTER 7

FINDING TRUTH

The previous January, my father had driven me back to Oglesby after Christmas break, the first time I'd been alone with him since I was twelve years old. Usually my mother would have driven me, but she had the flu. It was dark as we crossed the Illinois River and began the climb up the hill into Oglesby. My father broke what had become a long silence between us.

"Do you like it when boys put their hands in your pants?"

Involuntarily, I squeezed against the door. "Yeah, I do." Not that it's any of your business, I thought. I stared out the window, glad to see the lights of the A&W. I was almost home.

In August, 1971, my parents invited me to go with them to Craig's wedding in New York City. Craig had moved to Connecticut, where he helicoptered executives around the city. Especially after my father's question in January, the invitation to spend two weeks with Mom and him without a means of escape gave me pause. But last year's trip to New York had whetted my appetite for travel, and they were going to drive through Canada on the way out, through Windsor to Montreal, and down through New England, before attending the wedding in Queens.

My wanderlust overcame my reluctance, and I said good-bye to Jerry, expecting it to be the end of our relationship. I would have only a few days after the trip before I moved to Champaign.

My parents and I traveled in their truck, fitted with beds in the back under a truck-bed enclosure. On the second day of the trip, my father surprised me. "If you see someplace you want to stop, let me know. This is your trip, too."

"Okay, I'll do that."

But I wasn't all that focused on the sights of the countryside or of the French city of Montreal. Though I did ask to stop at a couple of stores, my thoughts kept turning to Jerry. I wrote increasingly romantic letters, declaring my love for him. Two weeks apart catalyzed my feelings.

When we heard the day after the wedding that my grandmother had died, we rushed back, driving straight through. I dropped my parents off at the farm and, heart racing, went on to La Salle to see Jerry, unsure of my reception.

He was painting the outside of the house when I pulled up.

"Karen! You're back." He put his brush down and wrapped his arms around me. Mingled with the turpentine odor was his familiar summer smell.

"I love you." I tightened my arms around him, oblivious to his paint-splattered T-shirt.

"I love you, too, you dummy!" Seeing his silly grin slowed my pulse.

A few days later, we began a long-distance romance.

It was a hot August day when my sister Nancy and Mom drove me and my sparse belongings down to Champaign. As we pulled up to Leeman Lodge, a three-story rooming house, I felt a surge of hope. Maybe here is where life will get better. If the future I was beginning to imagine with Jerry didn't work out, there'd be lots of other guys on campus. We gathered my things, including my prized typewriter that I'd earned by walking beans (cutting out weeds) on the farm. The downstairs common rooms were dark, but the large window in my twelve-by-twelve triple room at the top of the stairs brightened that space. Someone's jacket already lay on the single bed. The bunk beds looked solid enough, nicer than the army surplus bunks Nancy and I had used in my last years at home. The three chests and desks showed marks of age, but they were solid wood.

Nancy sat on the bottom bunk and chuckled. "This mattress sure is thicker than those army ones."

"Yeah, they'll be fine." I was eager for them to leave so I could explore the campus. Mom had packed a lunch, and after we ate the sandwiches, they left me on my own.

The wind rustled the tall trees on John Street as I walked past fraternity houses, a soaring Presbyterian church, the Jewish Hillel Foundation, a small grocery store, and the university student services building. After three blocks, I reached the quad, a central, park-like area surrounded by the original university buildings.

I sat on the grass, leaning against a tree, near the English building. I'd picked the U of I not only because it was the best public university in Illinois, but also because of the classic architecture with its red bricks and white shutters, ornamented with great swaths of cornice with dentil trim. Having explored the Illini Union on a campus visit, I knew that building, at the north end of the quad, was full of real hardwood paneling as if it were a country mansion. The sun began to settle below the horizon then, and the Union glowed in the golden light. I was a long way from the cornfields.

When I returned to Leeman Lodge, the room-mate who'd claimed the single bed was kneeling next to it on the floor. She had long brown hair, lively brown eyes, and a full mouth. She glanced up and smiled.

"Hi, I'm Mercedes. I'm praying. I'll be with you in twenty minutes."

"I'm Karen." She probably saw my face fall before I ducked behind the chest that separated her bed from the bunks. I sat on the lower bunk, my head in my hands. Praying, huh? Right.

Jerry had warned me about those "Jesus freaks." He'd gone up to DeKalb, to Northern Illinois University, to sell some handmade ceramic incense burners to the head shops. The Jesus freaks had accosted him and wouldn't stop bothering him.

Though he'd also been raised a Catholic, like me, he had stopped going to mass. Neither of us thought Jesus had anything to offer us. I had, however, intensified my search for truth since that suicidal crisis on the day I first talked to Jerry. I had not yet heard "You shall know the truth and the truth will set you free," but I instinctively longed to know what reality was solid enough to build a life on. But I was sure Jesus wasn't it.

I lay back on the bed. The years of dust accumulated in the wooden floor boards gave the room a stale air. I took a deep breath. I must have fallen asleep because I awoke to hear Mercedes and another girl talking softly. With the chest between us, I only picked up an occasional word: Jesus, God, love, faith.

Turns out, Mercedes and Cindy—that was my other roommate—had decided to live together that semester to talk about Jesus. Mercedes was a psychology major from Puerto Rico and a strong Christian. Cindy, a petite blonde who'd grown up in Urbana, studied sociology and struggled with her faith. After six weeks of listening to their conversations, I began to wonder about Jesus. They talked about him as if he was really there with them. Sometimes I heard them pray together. I'd never heard anything but rote Catholic prayers. Their prayers sounded more like a one-sided conversation.

One Friday night, I overhead Mercedes praying for Cindy's school work. "Lord, please help Cindy with her Chaucer paper."

"Oh, Lord, please help me." Cindy added her own plea.

I was seated at my desk, my back to them. When they finished, I turned my chair around and faced them. They were sitting, one on each end, on Mercedes's bed.

I stared at them. "Uh, do you really think God will help you with writing papers?"

"Oh, yeah," Mercedes replied. "I was so stuck, last semester, on my philosophy of social science paper. In the library one day, I prayed and started writing. Before I knew it, I'd written the whole thing, and it all made sense."

"Really?" That seemed a little too good to be true—God stooping down to write college term papers.

"Maybe it sounds a little too good to be true. But it is true!"

"If you say so." I bit the inside of my lip. How did she know what I was thinking?

"Maybe you'd like to go with us to Milton and Georgia's Sunday night." Mercedes smiled at me and Cindy nodded.

I knew they went to twice monthly discussion meetings on Sunday nights at these philosophy professors' house. After the meetings, they usually talked far into the night in our room. I'd overheard those discussions, of course, but I hadn't participated.

"Maybe." Just showing up at a meeting like that seemed like a big commitment.

"They live in a neat house in the woods, and Georgia always puts out good snacks. Last time, she had big strawberries." Cindy stood and put on her jacket. "Just think about it, okay? It's just a place to ask questions."

"We'll see." I turned back to my books. Maybe I would go. Without my realizing it, the water of the Word had begun to penetrate my dry heart as I overheard my roommates' conversations. The way they talked about God was a new idea to me. As a child in the Catholic Church, I'd gained a sense of God's majesty, but not of his friendship. God, if he was even knowable, seemed just like my father: cold, distant, remote.

I did go to Milton and Georgia's discussion group that Sunday night. They both taught philosophy. He at the university, she at the junior college. We gathered in their large living room in front of floor-to-ceiling bookcases flanking a stone fireplace. The attendees were a mix of students and townspeople. Some were professionals, whereas some of them were only marginally employed. At the end of the time, Milton asked if anyone wanted prayer. Like

Mercedes and Cindy, he prayed as if God was really listening to the needs—from jobs to exams.

The first few times, I listened silently. Finally, though, one night, in mid-November, a question pushed through my resistance. "How do you know the Bible is true?" I asked.

"Well, how do we know anything is true?" Milton stood with his back to a sparkling fire as we lounged in sofas and chairs in a semi-circle around him. "We look for evidence." He told a long story of a person who'd set out to investigate the backgrounds of the biblical writing, intending to disprove them, but eventually deciding they were really true.

"Well, okay. But the Resurrection seems the most unbelievable. How do you know about that?" I reached for a chocolate-covered strawberry. Georgia smiled at me from across the group.

"There are lots of sources of knowledge about that. One of the most compelling, though, is what the disciples did. They were uneducated fishermen who turned the world upside down."

"Well, yeah, I see your point." It was time to go then. As we said our goodbyes under the starry night, I wondered.

Back at my room, I called Jerry, pulling the phone cord into the closet for privacy. Mercedes and Cindy had both settled at their desks when we returned from the group. After we discussed when he'd be down to pick me up for Thanksgiving break next week, I told him about going to the discussion group. Jerry and I had occasionally discussed religion during the semester, but we hadn't reached any conclusions. After a few minutes, I spoke a thought that popped into my mind: "What if God has put me here to know him?"

"What if Satan has put you there to mislead you?" Jerry's response was quick. I changed the subject, and, after a little more chit-chat, we hung up. But I lay in my upper bunk for a long time before sleep.

Another conflict with Jerry. He usually visited every weekend. But he'd not come down this weekend. He said he had to study, but I wondered. We'd had a rough time last week. He'd recently bought a 1964 VW Van from his landlord and had driven it down for the first time a week ago. It had been parked on the street in twenty degree weather. When we'd wanted to go to a movie Saturday evening, it wouldn't start.

"Sometimes it doesn't start very well when it's cold," Jerry said. He climbed out the driver's side.

"What can it be?" I pulled my coat tighter as I leaned toward him.

Jerry stood, holding the door open. "I don't know exactly."

"The ignition? Maybe it's broken."

"No, it turns over."

"What about the fuel line?"

"I don't think so." Jerry frowned, but I kept suggesting possibilities. Not that I worked on cars, but I grew up with brothers who did.

When I suggested checking the battery, Jerry exploded. "The battery is fine! I checked it last week. Will you just let me work on this?" He slammed the door, stalked to the back of the van, and jerked open the engine compartment.

Why does he get so mad at me? I'm just trying to help. I found an old blanket in the back seat and wrapped up to wait.

After twenty minutes, he got the van running. When he climbed back into the driver's side, I slid over to him and put my hand on his thigh. He stiffened.

"It's too late for the movie, and I'm freezing. Mercedes and Cindy are out. Let's go warm up."

We'd done more than warm up. Still afraid of pregnancy and embarrassed to go to a doctor for birth control, I used all the sexual techniques I knew short of intercourse to bring him round after that conflict. Even so, when we'd parted the next day, he was still a little miffed.

He'd seemed okay in our phone conversations this week, but maybe he wasn't over his anger yet, and that's really why he didn't come down this weekend. I turned my face to the wall and took a deep breath. I hated conflict. I felt ashamed, like something was wrong with me that I couldn't keep him happy.

Mercedes and Cindy had been studying quietly, but now they gathered their bath supplies and went out the door. All five rooms on the second floor shared a large bathroom at the end of the hall. I threw off my covers, gathered my own toiletries, and followed them.

Stepping into the shower, I thought, Jerry is the best thing that's ever happened to me. With unaccustomed firmness, I said to myself, I am not gonna mess this up. I will keep my mouth shut. He's not stupid. I'm the one that's stupid. He loves me. I love him. I can't lose him. I can't. As I turned on the warm shower water, hot tears sprang to my eyes. I scrubbed as if my shame could be rubbed off if only I pressed hard enough.

Neither Jerry nor I brought the conflict up again. He resumed his weekly visits through the fall of 1971. We enjoyed each other even more as I worked on trusting his judgment. We liked the outdoors, arts and crafts, and laughing at life's absurdities. We began to plan for a future together.

At Christmas break he picked me up in the Mustang he still owned and took me back to the farm. He was on break, too, from his data processing studies at the junior college where we'd met. On December 23, in the drafty old kitchen with my parents and brother, Henry (who was still in high school), Jerry and I were eating lunch at the metal kitchen table we'd had since I was little. I felt much safer around my father when Jerry was there. Jerry knew something of the abuse, but I hadn't gone into much detail. I tried not to think about it.

After lunch, Jerry touched my hand. "Let's go Christmas shopping in Ottawa. I still have a couple of gifts to get."

"Okay, that sounds fun." I got up to get my coat.

Henry asked, "Can I go too?"

"No, not this time." That seemed odd. He had gone with us last week to Oswego. But I was keeping my mouth shut.

When we finished our shopping in Ottawa, Jerry drove south out of town. "Let's go for a drive." I was always up for an afternoon car ride. Among the many painful childhood memories, our aimless Sunday drives stood out like a daffodil in January. We followed the curves of Illinois 71 next to the half-frozen Illinois River. Speeding along the water in our small bass-tracker boat was another daffodil memory from my childhood. Now, we followed the waterway toward Starved Rock State Park.

At Illinois 178, we turned south and Jerry pulled into Matthiessen State Park. On our second date we'd hiked for miles here. We parked the car and walked out into the woods. I pulled my light jacket tighter. The oaks swayed above us, and snow frosted the pines around us. We walked toward the trails. Halfway across a wide wooden bridge, Jerry stopped and faced me.

He took my hand. "Will you marry me?"

"Oh, yes!" He pulled me into his arms. "That's why you didn't want Henry along!" I pulled away and grinned at him. "I didn't think you'd actually ask. I thought it would just happen."

Hand in hand, we walked back to the Mustang. He opened the door for me. "Today is your parent's anniversary, isn't it?" I asked as I stepped into the car.

"Yup." We grinned at each other.

Jerry's proposal softened my heart toward God. Was God giving me Jerry? One night in mid-January, near the end of break, I lay in my grandmother's old room, which was now the guest room. I preferred the regular mattress there rather than the thin army ones in my old bedroom. I snuggled into the worn sheet and the warm wool blanket. I put my hands behind my head, settling into the pillow. The room still smelled faintly of urine. Grandma had just died the previous summer. At the end of this iron bedstead, Henry and I had lain as she had read comic books to us. Though she smiled little, she responded to my fears and provided some comfort. I'd run to this bed when I felt afraid of monsters, and Grandma had tucked me in. My mind wandered until I was captured by a thought that suddenly came in loud and clear: If Jesus rose from the dead, He's still alive.

Oh, that's right! Aloud, I said: "Jesus, if you're there, I want to know about it." Immediately, I sensed I wasn't alone. I took a deep breath. I sat up in bed, pulling my knees to my chest. "You are real!"

Grace had brought me to that point of openness. Then, I had no idea of the damage my father had done. I didn't realize I felt like an object rather than a person. I didn't know my core of worthlessness. And I had no clue of the emotional battles God would lead me through before I was finally free of that shame. But Jesus had taken my hand.

PART II
BLESSED
WRESTLING

CHAPTER 8

BREAKING DOWN

When I opened myself to Jesus that night in my grandmother's bedroom, rain began to fall on my desert, though the soil was so sandy, little moisture was absorbed. But the drops of God's grace that soaked in supported new growth.

I began to trust Jerry a bit more. As he felt less controlled, he was intrigued by the changes in me. Mercedes worked for Campus Crusade for Christ. One weekend we visited her at her office, and she handed him a *Four Spiritual Laws* booklet. Back in La Salle, he laid it on his nightstand. Night after night, he told me, God nudged him. Finally, one night he read it, understood the gospel, and responded to Jesus' invitation.

On June 10, 1972, Jerry and I were married in a simple Catholic ceremony in Halesburg. My mother's irises adorned the altar, my grandmother's crochet trimmed the chiffon gown I sewed, and a cousin baked and decorated the wedding cake. Libby and Ed, Jerry's parents, welcomed their first daughter-in-law into their family. We held the outdoor reception at the farm, under perfect skies. When we pulled out of the gravel driveway in our Volkswagen bus for our camping honeymoon, I felt safe and whole for the first time in my life.

I was safe with Jerry, but real wholeness was years in the future. Together, we began to pursue that wholeness at Urbana Assembly of God (UAG). In the seventies, it was a vibrant, prophetic church. Richard Foth had been called as its first pastor in the late sixties as the charismatic renewal swept through America.

Pastor Foth taught us and learned with us, who Jesus was and who we are. We rejoiced through every church service, including Sunday and Wednesday evenings. Having never sung the great hymns of the Protestant church, I thrilled to the sounds and lyrics of "At the Cross," "Amazing Love," and "Oh for a Thousand Tongues to Sing." I soaked up truth. I thirsted after life. I longed to see the face of God. Psalm 27:4 was one of my favorites: "One thing I ask of the Lord, this is what I seek: that I may dwell in the house of the Lord all the days of my life, to gaze upon the beauty of the Lord and to seek him in his temple."

Jerry developed his pottery. I clerked at a fabric store. But our lives revolved around UAG, full of young, growing Christians. In the intimacy of the Holy Spirit, we shared personal prayer requests in the Sunday evening meetings of several hundred.

Pastor Foth's public prayers began to heal my dry heart. Beginning a service, he often prayed: "We're a needy people." In that prayer I claimed my own neediness. A regular dismissal prayer: "This is the day you have made, we will rejoice in it." Rejoicing began to replace despair. He preached "the ground is level at the foot of the cross." I took my place, one of many who belonged there. He said, "Inside, we're all just little boys and little girls." For the first time, I felt God's fathering in Pastor Foth's prayers. Instead of needing to be strong, I was allowed to be weak.

He brought in great men and women of missions, like Charles Greenaway, then foreign missions secretary for the Assemblies of God denomination. I'll never forget that tall, heavyset man preaching from the story of Shadrach, Meshach, and Abednego. Though the king threatened to throw them into the fiery furnace, these three Hebrew men would not bow down before the king's idol. They told the king that God would rescue them. "But even if he does not, we want you to know, O king, that we will not serve your gods or worship the image of gold you have set up" (Dan 3:18). When they were hauled into the fire, the king rose to stare at the sight, not of burned bodies, but of four living persons walking amid the flames. God himself had come to their rescue. The king called for their release and promoted them.

Reverend Greenaway summarized the story: "Our God can, our God will, and, if not, he has something better." In that sentence, I got a glimmer of the power and love of God.

Dick Foth was a humble man, and he represented that redeeming God. One day when the church was building an addition to house a small school, I saw his emotional stability. On each side of a hallway, a large room was meant to be temporarily divided into two with flexible wall dividers. When he walked into the south room, the workers were half done with a concrete block wall dividing the space. He stopped, grunted, and said little. I watched him. I knew my father's rage. He turned on his heel and walked away. "I guess we have a concrete wall." I followed him, amazed at his response. His calmness conveyed God's calmness.

When I unexpectedly became pregnant in the fall of 1974, I was distressed. At a Sunday night service, near the end of the pregnancy, the wife of our associate pastor, herself pregnant, sat next to me. "God knows what he's doing," she said. Though I was less sure, her faith watered my own. In three years of walking with God and sitting under Dick's teaching, I had begun to sprout a little groundcover of faith. But this momentous change in our lives threatened to uproot the baby plants.

On June 24, 1975, I was ten days past my due date. Finally, that morning, I studied my bloated face in the mirror. "Okay, God, I accept whatever happens." Not like I had any viable choices; however, I did have the choice to emotionally fight the reality of impending motherhood. That morning, I stopped fighting. In the evening, my water broke.

By the next evening, after a medically uneventful labor, Jennifer was born. She was sweet and beautiful. After three days in the hospital, we took her home. Jerry sold his pottery at an art fair that weekend. Jerry's mom Libby, a grade school teacher, came down to help Jerry, while I stayed home to care for Jenny.

I had been nursing Jenny in her room off the living room of our small house when I heard the front door open. Picking up Jenny, I stepped into the living room in time to see Jerry collapse on a bean bag chair while Libby sank into a director's chair next to him.

"Jerry, your face is so red. What's wrong?" I raised my eyebrows at Libby when he didn't respond.

"Get him some water." Libby pointed at the kitchen. "He's overheated. We sat in the sun all afternoon." My heart pulsed in my ears. Libby never spoke so forcefully. Jenny began howling as I rushed to get a glass of water. I'd never seen Jerry look so dry. He seemed disoriented. Thankfully, after a few hours rest, his temperature returned to normal.

The heat persisted, though, during the next few days and nights. Without air conditioning our little house never cooled down, so between the heat and feeding Jenny, I got little sleep. Also my post-childbirth hormones were raging. And my emotional denial about the abuse was crumbling. The stress would have been manageable except for predisposition to mental illness that ran in my family. At the time, though, I knew none of that. On the afternoon of the tenth day postpartum, I was nursing Jenny while Jerry was glazing pots in the garage studio, getting ready for our next art fair. I didn't think I needed any help with Jenny, so I'd sent Libby home after her help at the art fair the weekend before.

Suddenly a thought popped into my mind: Jennifer will be tortured and killed for Jesus. I flinched at the image in my head of a teenage Jennifer stretched out on a medieval rack being torn apart. I burst into tears. "No! I can't take anymore." I cried as I got up and put Jenny in her crib. She screamed. Wiping my eyes, I ran out of the nursery.

Several times in the last few days, I had sensed God speaking to me about the terrible things this little baby faced. I needed Jerry to hold me. When would he be done? I can't tell him what God is saying. It would be too much for him. And I can't bother him while he's working. He'll be mad.

Within half an hour, Jerry came in and calmed us both down. He wasn't mad. But I noticed him staring at me as I fried hamburgers for dinner.

I slept some that night, but at 5 A.M. I was wide awake. "Jerry! Wake up!" I shook his shoulder. He rolled over, frowning.

"What, Karen?"

"You know those bad thoughts I've been having? God's getting rid of them, all the evil. It's the last contraction. It'll all be gone." I grinned as I jumped up. "I'm free!"

"Karen. It's 5:00 in the morning. Calm down." His puzzled frown didn't register with me.

"No, don't you see? Nothing is wrong with me!" I danced around the bed.

"Go in the other room, Karen. I need to sleep."

By the end of the next day, a Sunday, I had completely lost my tenuous grip on reality. By 5:30, when we would normally have been preparing to go to evening worship, I had collapsed on the nursery floor, my toes curled around the leg of the wooden crib. Only that leg felt real to me. My mood had switched from exhilaration to terror, and I was paralyzed with fear of what the future held for Jenny and me. But I could not speak of the terror.

Jerry gathered Jenny and me and drove us out to the church to get help. He'd never seen me like this before. When he pulled up, he rushed in, leaving me with Jenny. Gloria, a friend, came out and climbed in beside me.

"What did he say?" I asked. Gloria took Jenny from my arms.

"He said, 'Karen's mind is fried.'" She smiled at me and stroked Jenny's arm.

"She's so beautiful, Karen. You'll be okay. Lots of new moms have a little trouble."

But I was having more than a little trouble. I was having a postpartum psychosis. Many women work through a depression after childbirth, but less than 1% of new mothers actually lose touch with everyday reality.

That Sunday evening, though, Jerry had no idea what was going on. Thinking I just needed some reassurance, he asked Dick to come see me after the evening service. On the way home from the church, Jerry purchased Similac to feed Jenny. Back home,

I sprawled in the beanbag chair while he tried to calm Jennifer's agitation. She was used to nursing and balked at the bottle.

When Dick and his wife Ruth arrived later that evening, I was crying, and Jerry was pacing the floor with the screaming Jennifer. Ruth took our bewildered newborn from Jerry, and they all went to the kitchen. Ruth's calmness soon calmed Jenny.

Dick lowered himself into the beanbag chair next to mine.

"What's going on, Karen?" I stared at his kind eyes. His fatherly presence sparked old memories, and I blurted out the old pain I'd kept covered up for twenty years.

"My father molested me. Lots of times. I could never be alone with him." I wrapped my arms around my midsection doubling over.

"How old were you?"

"Four years old, eight years old, twelve years old. Lots of times."

"Does Jerry know?"

"Yes."

"I'm so sorry, Karen. It wasn't your fault. You were just a little girl. Your dad is responsible, not you."

"No, I'm a bad person. I'm evil. Jenny is going to be tortured because I'm so bad."

Dick, seeing I needed more than reassurance, suggested taking me to see our doctor in the morning. They took Jenny overnight so we could get some sleep.

The next morning, after a brief exam, my doctor sent me to the psychiatrist down the hall. His questions barely registered. I didn't know where I was, what day of the week it was, or who the president was. He prescribed Thorazine, a powerful antipsychotic drug, and I was hospitalized. After ten days of confinement, I was released to Jerry's care. I was still on Thorazine and now also imipramine, an antidepressant. The drugs had ameliorated the worst of the symptoms, and I knew who Jerry and Libby were. While I was hospitalized, Libby had come to help with Jenny. I don't know how we'd have managed without her because I took little note of Jenny. Libby, however, delighted in her only grandchild, even as she worried about her daughter-in-law.

When I was at my worst, Dick Foth treated me as if I were at my best. He visited me often. Some days he just sat by the side of the couch and smiled at me when I couldn't pull myself upright. Other days, he paced with me around the living room, letting me put my hand in the crook of his elbow.

One day, as we were pacing. I said something humorous. Dick laughed. "You're a funny lady."

"You mean, when I'm normal, when I'm okay." I couldn't believe he thought I was funny, right then. Only sane people were funny. I knew I wasn't thinking straight, which was progress, because when I was really psychotic, I didn't know how bad off I was.

"No, I mean right now . . . you're witty."

I could not recall anything positive my parents had ever said about me. His affirmation, in the midst of the worst time of my life, was an infusion of nutrients to my dry, sandy, soil.

Two weeks after I was released, Pastor Foth called for an afternoon of prayer for me and for two others who were having serious problems. By this time the medication had pulled me back to everyday reality, but fear still gripped me. I was especially terrified, in my more lucid moments, that I would never be normal again. That afternoon, as dozens of brothers and sisters beseeched God for my healing, God calmed that terror. For the first time, I believed God would heal me. I caught a glimpse of myself in a green garden festooned with pink roses.

In the next few months, many people from church spent time with me, giving me hugs and kind words. By September, when Jenny was three months old, I was able to attend a baby shower. I saw only compassion and concern in their eyes as the women from the church showered me with gifts and words of parenting wisdom.

By then, after eight weeks of caring for Jenny, Libby had returned to teaching. We went on public aid so Jerry could take care of me. He got a vasectomy—we were not risking this kind of reaction again. Jenny would be an only child.

I'd quit the fabric store before Jenny was born, and I now stayed home to care for her. My fears were less extreme, though still distressing. I no longer believed Jennifer would be tortured, but I still struggled. Sandy, a homemaker from Family Service, spent several hours a week teaching me mothering. She had three teenage daughters. One morning, cleaning the toaster, I spoke a fear. "What if Jenny doesn't like me?"

"You're her mom. Of course she'll like you."

I felt reassured. Sandy reported fun shopping trips with her girls. I had never done fun trips with my mom, but Sandy's relationship with her daughters gave me hope. I was beginning to be able to incorporate other's reassurance rather than focus only on my own fearful thoughts.

Though the emotional extremes of a psychotic episode receded, the crisis had exposed the weeds of unforgiveness in my dry heart. God confronted me with the parable of the unjust steward. In Matthew 18, Jesus tells of a servant who owed his master so much money that he could never repay it. When the steward begged to be released from the debt, the Master released him.

The steward, however, turned around and threw into jail a man who owed him a few dollars, intending to keep him there until he'd paid the last cent.

When his master heard of the injustice, he threw the steward to the torturers. "You wicked servant, I canceled all that debt of yours because you begged me to. Shouldn't you have had mercy on your fellow servant just as I had on you?" Jesus' reflection on this story penetrated my heart: "This is how my heavenly Father will treat each of you unless you forgive your brother from your heart."

I knew God was asking me to forgive my father the abuse. But how could I forgive him? In the year or two after Jenn's birth, images of him pulling my pants down dogged my daily life. Brought to light by the psychotic break, the flashbacks repulsed me. Sex, particularly, was fraught with intrusive memories. Like many abuse victims, I'd used sex to attract a man, but was less interested after the wedding. Sex had felt powerful before. Now my husband's touch felt too much like my father's violations. Jerry, though, kept saying, "I don't want to hurt you."

Though he was frustrated many times, he remained engaged with me.

And he was a wonderful, playful father to Jenny. Jerry often held Jenny on his lap, reading Richard Scarry books to her. I knew my own father had never given me that kind of affection. Even if he'd wanted to, I'd have resisted because of the lesson I'd learned in the cornfield. My father's lap was not safe. How could I forgive that?

CHAPTER 9

BREAKING THROUGH

"Free at last, thank God Almighty, I'm free at last!" My friend Kathy slapped the steering wheel as she pulled into the traffic on Interstate 57 just south of Champaign-Urbana. I wasn't familiar with Dr. Martin Luther King Jr.'s epitaph, but I echoed the feeling. I had adjusted to being a stay-at-home mom, but I was grateful for a few days of freedom. Kathy and I were on our way to a big charismatic conference in Kansas City in July of 1977. We were going to stay with Kathy's friends in Lawrence. I was so excited. Jenny had gone to Libby's for the ten days and Jerry had stayed in Urbana to work. We'd been on public aid for only a few months before he'd begun working with a small electrical contracting company.

By Christmas of 1975, I was fully recovered from the postpartum crisis. I'd been on medication for only a few months during the worst of it. I was functioning as a wife and mother. Before I'd gotten pregnant, I'd been involved in church drama. By Christmas of 1976, when Urbana Assembly produced the musical, *His Love Reaching,* I was well enough to create a mime to highlight the story. I'd lost my baby weight and stopped biting my fingernails. For me, those were all barometers of good emotional health. God had healed me.

We arrived in Lawrence, a couple of days before the conference, giving us time to relax. Kathy's friends lived in a big old house, with room for company in several upstairs bedrooms. I explored little shops in downtown Lawrence. We discussed the Bible with Kathy's friends, who were interested in missions.

I thought Jerry and I ought to be missionaries. Everyone at Urbana Assembly spoke so highly of them, and many of our friends had joined Youth with A Mission (YWAM), a worldwide missionary organization. In Amsterdam, where some of our friends had gone, YWAM operated from two large houseboats. Our good friend Pat had also gone to Amsterdam to live on the boats and work with their mime ministry. She had stopped to say good-bye the first Sunday after Jenny was born. I had so longed that day to trade places with her. Missions seemed glamorous and exciting. Motherhood seemed dull and boring. Though by now I'd accepted the responsibilities of motherhood and enjoyed watching Jenny's growth, going to YWAM still felt like more fun.

When the conference started, I soaked up the sermons from teachers like Derek Prince, Charles Simpson, and Bob Mumford. One afternoon, Mr. Mumford spoke in Kemper Arena to a crowd of twenty thousand. He said God was preparing us for heaven, where we will be "safe, innocent, and happy." I was so grateful and excited by his message that I jumped out of my seat and ran across the empty floor to the tall platform where he stood, receiving the applause.

"Thank you!" I called up to him.

He glanced at me, clearly puzzled. I returned to my seat, thrilled I'd gotten a chance to speak to him. Kathy gave me an odd look, but said nothing.

God had healed me, I was sure of that. It didn't occur to me that this excitement was over-the-top, the beginning of another psychotic episode. I thought God was speaking to me. I'd never felt safe, innocent, or happy. God was telling me he would remake me, starting at the beginning. Only children were innocent, weren't they? I got to be a little girl again.

But, as I began to think like a little girl, I sank into the old feelings of abandonment. After two days of increasing internal conflict, those old feelings intensified the battles.

One night, I lay in the darkness alone, waiting for sleep. The unfamiliar bedroom threw odd shadows from the streetlights. I couldn't place the smell that lingered in the room. I was exhausted after a long day of meetings, but I didn't feel sleepy. I began to imagine myself in Amsterdam, with Pat, living on the houseboats. I loved the smell of the sea. It reminded me of some of my best childhood memories of speeding on the river. Just as I began to imagine the gentle swelling of the waves that would rock the Amsterdam houseboat, I thought I felt another movement, as if God himself grabbed hold of me. I saw myself being shaped into a large ball in his great, rough hands.

It was my father all over again. I'm only an object to God, too. I felt him throw me. I felt myself sailing through empty space, out among the planets, though no stars lit the way. Only dark terror surrounded me, as I lost all sense of where or who I was. I screamed.

The bedroom door flew open, throwing light from the hall into the room's darkness. Kathy ran in. "Karen, what's wrong?"

"God is throwing me away." I rolled into a fetal position, facing the wall.

"Throwing you . . . Oh, Karen, I think you're in trouble again." She touched my shoulder.

After my inappropriate thank-you to Bob Mumford, my behavior had grown increasingly bizarre. The day before, we'd gone to a luncheon gathering at a church hall. Several hundred people attended, including Derek Prince. Sandwiches, fruit, and chips were set up buffet style, and groups of people stood eating with plates in their hands. I was already in a full-fledged manic psychotic episode—I thought I'd actually died and gone to heaven.

At one point, as I observed people streaming into the foyer, I noticed a thin, gray-haired man who I thought was Mr. Leonard, from junior college. I pushed my way through the crowd and threw my arms around him. "Mr. Leonard. I'm so glad you're here, in heaven!"

He patted my back before taking my shoulders and holding me off. "I think you've confused me with someone else." His perplexed look was lost on me.

I turned away, pulled by my ricocheting delusions. A new thought had pushed itself to the front of my disordered mind: Maybe you and Jerry and Jenny are Elijah. The Elijah family. I have to ask Mr. Prince about that. He was standing in the middle of the fellowship hall, the center of a group. I tugged on his sleeve. "Do you think I could be Elijah?" I asked. He tilted his head and stared at me. "What? I'm busy here."

"Oh, sorry." His rebuke registered. I noticed Kathy staring at me, frowning. She approached me, taking my arm to lead me to a folding chair on the edge of the room. I followed her, vaguely aware of something wrong. I didn't tell her what I was thinking about being Elijah.

But, tonight, the hallucination of being thrown out into an empty universe was a complete mood swing. Not only was I not Elijah, I was trash. As I lay with my knees pulled to my chest, Kathy squeezed my shoulder. "We need to call Jerry." In a few minutes, she called me to the phone.

"What happened, Karen?" Jerry asked, blowing out a deep breath.

"I don't know." I knew who he was and, in a moment of lucidity, I knew Kathy was right. I was again descending into madness. Jerry flew out to drive back with us and took me straight to the psychiatric ward. This time, a different psychiatrist diagnosed manic depression and prescribed Mellaril, another antipsychotic drug. Again, after a ten-day hospitalization, I was released to Jerry's care. I had almost stopped eating in the hospital, dropping ten pounds in ten days. Jenny was still at Libby and Ed's.

My first night at home again, I couldn't sleep. My mood switched from high to low without warning. At midnight, the thought popped into my mind:

"You're the Anti-Christ. You're the Anti-Christ, and you're alone on the earth." I patted Jerry's back.

"What, Karen?" He rolled over, frowning.

"Nothing. Just wanted to be sure you were there."

"I'm right here. And I need to sleep." He rolled away from me.

I jumped out of bed. I ran through the dark house. Alone. Abandoned. Evil.

I bumped into the kitchen door frame. The light went on in our bedroom and Jerry appeared. "Karen. What is going on?" He held out his hand as he walked toward me.

"I'm terrible." My eyes darted from his face to dark shapes of the beanbag chairs in the corner. Maybe I could hide in them.

"I'm right here, Karen. Let me get you a glass of milk." He sat me at the kitchen table. With his back to me, he reached into the cupboard over the stove before he opened the refrigerator and poured a glass of milk.

"Here, drink this."

I gulped it down. Something tasted bitter. "Yuk, what's that?" I said, peering at the green sludge at the bottom of the glass.

"The milk must be bad, I guess. Let's go back to bed."

I let him lead me into the bedroom.

"Go to sleep, Karen."

"I'll try."

I was able to go back to sleep. The bitterness in the bottom of the milk had been an extra dose of Mellaril Jerry had slipped in. After the psychiatrist upped the dosage the next day, the delusions eased.

Three weeks after my release, we picked up two-year-old Jenny in Streator. She clung to Jerry, but when I held out my arms to her she turned away. Sandy, who'd reassured me the baby would like me, was wrong. Even my own child rejected me.

Mercedes, who'd been gone for a few years, had moved back to town. The Saturday after Jenny came back from her grandma and grandpa's, Mercedes spent an afternoon with us, playing in a local park and taking photos. Though by then the voices and delusions were less insistent, I was still very fragile. I took Jenny's continuing preference for Jerry personally. Jerry was doing all the cooking, laundry, and childcare. I did well to get a shower.

After we had supper together that evening, Mercedes was washing the dishes while I sat at the table. On the floor, Jenny played with her

Fisher-Price dollhouse. Jerry had gone to the garage. Mercedes spread out a cloth on the table. She picked up the rinsed glasses and placed them upside down on the cloth. She looked at me. "You're not messing just with your mind; you're messing with your marriage!"

"What do you mean?" A jolt of fear paralyzed me.

"I mean Jerry told me he's getting tired of doing all the work. And he was embarrassed today when you hugged Ann at the grocery store. You don't usually do that. He says you could snap out of it if you wanted to."

"Do you think I can 'snap out of it'?"

"Maybe not just like that." She snapped her finger. "But I think you can exert a little more control, don't you?"

She was right. I could work harder at controlling my unusual behavior and participating in household chores. In the ensuing days, as I exerted the control I did have, God gave me more. I began to get out of bed by 8 A.M. I prepared Jerry's lunch. I helped wash dishes.

And I sought counseling. We were so poor I attended only a couple of sessions, but one thing I heard in that office began to change my life. After I'd talked to the counselor he had called Jerry in alone to ask a few questions. Another therapist shared the waiting room. As I was pacing around the small space, the other therapist opened his door. He smiled at me as he sat down at the reception desk. He looked like a professor with his white hair and tweed jacket. When I didn't stop pacing, he looked up from his notepad and said,

"Therefore, there is now no condemnation for those who are in Christ Jesus." He was quoting Roman 8:1 to me, which I knew, but had never heard with my heart.

"Yes. Thank you." I sat down.

He smiled at me again before returning to his notes.

For the first time, it sank in that God was not angry with me. Pastor Foth's teaching on God's grace and love had softened my soil. And that day, in that nondescript room, in Huntington Towers in Champaign, Illinois, God himself planted an oak: "No condemnation. I am not throwing you away." In the sandy soil of my heart, he established an oasis.

The deep sense of rejection I felt because of my father's sin against me had helped precipitate the terrifying hallucination of being thrown away. The lie was this: "If my father rejects me, my heavenly Father will reject me, too." But what I truly heard that day for the first time was: "Though your father rejected you, I accept you." I began to grasp Psalm

27:10: "Though my father . . . forsake me, the Lord will receive me."

In that oasis, I asked God why I'd developed such serious emotional difficulties. Over the next year, I kept asking. Near the end of 1978, I again read the parable of the unforgiving servant in Matthew 18. Again God confronted me about forgiveness, and this time I made a deep choice to forgive my father's abuse, though the process took years to finalize. I knew I never wanted to return to that torturer's den. "This is how my heavenly Father will treat each of you unless you forgive your brother from your heart."

God himself seemed to be saying, *Here it is. Your emotional crises are that torturer's den. Unforgiveness is the issue.* This time I knew the voice in my head really was God. Forgiveness was scriptural. By this time, I was participating in a weekly fellowship time, keeping the household running, and looking after Jenny. Unlike my psychotic days, I knew who the president was, who I was, and where I was. I felt God's real, specific conviction of my unforgiveness.

Abandonment and abuse do not always result in hearing voices and seeing things that aren't there, as I experienced. My reactions were extreme. Scientific research points to a genetic predisposition to severe mental illness. I didn't know much about that at the time. I knew only that I'd gone through hell, I might go through hell again, and I was scared. In that year, I began to wrestle with God. Like Jacob wrestling with the angel, I did not intend to let him go until he blessed me. I would not give up. Though I'd been labeled "mental patient," I was determined to break through to the new identity God wanted to give me.

CHAPTER 10

ACCEPTING
GOD'S LOVE

J enny, are you ready?" I pulled on my jacket and went to check on three-year-old Jennifer in her room. The second bedroom of our 900-square-foot house, like the master bedroom, also opened off the living room. She was sitting on the hardwood floor, surrounded by dirty clothes, pulling on her jeans.

"How come you're not ready? I told you half an hour ago we were going to Prayer and Share this morning."

She looked up at me, her bottom lip quivering, but she didn't say anything.

I pulled her up and jerked her pants on. "Where's your coat? The red one Grandma gave you? We're going to be late."

"I dunno." She stood in the middle of the floor staring at me, a tear rolling down her cheek.

"I wish you'd hang it up. That's what these hooks are for, remember?" I looked around the room. The loft bed Jerry had built, with a built-in art desk underneath, was cluttered with paper, scissors, and colored pencils. Piles of clothes lay underneath. Richard Scarry books and a Fisher-Price farm set, among other toys and trash, obscured the floor. "You have so much stuff you can't even keep track of it all."

I thought of the bedroom I'd shared with my sister growing up. It was half this size. I noticed the doll Libby had sewn a wardrobe for, lying on its back near the window, the handmade clothes dusty on the floor. Nobody ever made doll clothes for me. And my father didn't put me to bed, either, not like her dad does. A jolt of jealousy shot through me. I had missed so much.

I wiped away a tear as I stared at a pile of clothing in the corner near the closet. A bit of red stuck out of the bottom.

"Is that your coat, over there?" I put both hands on Jenny's shoulders, turning her to face the corner.

"That's it." She ran to the corner and pulled it out. She wiped her cheek on the fake fur trim, then put her arms out. I helped her into it.

"You've got to clean the room Saturday. Do you hear me?"

"Okay, Mommy."

We hustled out the door, arriving ten minutes late to the meeting of women who had become my emotional lifeline since the breakdowns. Leaving Jenny at the nursery, I slipped into the circle of a dozen women. We met at the front of the 400-seat sanctuary, using several chairs and the front pew. I picked up the day's handout: Vulnerability. Judy, our thoughtful leader, always brought up challenging topics, though her kindness softened her intensity.

"Hi, Karen. We're just getting started." Judy nodded at me from across the circle. I skimmed over the paper. "Let go of your self-protections" jumped out at me. Who's going to protect me if I don't? Judy must have seen my face change. "Karen, do you have some thoughts about vulnerability?"

"Well, vulnerability is kind of a hard word. Vulnerable people get hurt. I think most of you know my father sexually abused me." I glanced around the group. Most of the women nodded. "Where was God when I was so vulnerable? I couldn't protect myself then, so I'm sure as heck gonna protect myself now." I crossed my arms over my chest and leaned back, staring at the floor. No one said anything for a minute. Just when I thought I'd committed a real faux pas, Sue, next to me, put her arm around me.

Judy's face softened. "Where is God when we suffer? That's one of the big questions, isn't it?"

"Yeah, I've been reading Philip Yancey, *Where is God When it Hurts?* What he seems to be saying is that God is right there, suffering with you.[2] Maybe. I can't see it, though."

"You've been through a lot, Karen. God has healed you of a lot. He'll help you with these questions, too. Everybody wrestles with the question of evil. It's hard to understand." Her calm smile calmed my heart.

"You can say that again." I glanced at her.

She held my eye for a moment.

"God loves you, Karen. Maybe you need to ask him to reveal his love to you."

"Yeah, I have been asking." I straightened in my chair and stared at the floor again.

Last week, she had taught on the three revelations, as she called them. First, there's the revelation of Jesus as Savior, then the revelation of the power of the Holy Spirit, and thirdly, the revelation of the love of the Father. She'd made the point that God needed to reveal each aspect of himself to us. She'd said we know God only by revelation.

Judy turned the discussion back to vulnerability then, but I wasn't listening. I could not make sense of why I'd been through so much suffering—either in childhood or in recent adulthood. But I knew I needed to forgive my father. And I guess God had the right to allow me to suffer in the breakdowns. My healing had glorified God. These women, indeed, the whole congregation, had praised God as they watched my recovery from such serious mental illness.

But a thousand questions swirled in my dry, dusty heart, including many I had not even put into words yet. After the meeting, I picked up Jenny and went home. I'd recently begun a sewing business, and a bridesmaid's dress needed finishing before Saturday. At least there was something I could do well. After we ate peanut butter and jelly sandwiches, I told Jenny she could play in my room while I sewed, until she got tired enough for her nap.

"Okay, Mommy!" She dragged her laundry basket, containing three dollies, into our bedroom, sliding the basket up to the mirror in the front of the closet door next to my sewing desk. I smiled at her. She grinned. Poor girl, I'm so hard on her, I thought, as I picked up the blue silk bodice piece.

I knew I expected too much from Jenny. I couldn't seem to help it. Therapy would have helped, but not only could we not afford it, that vulnerability required more trust than I had.

When Saturday came, I surveyed the mess in Jenny's room. It looked worse than it had on Tuesday morning. An open sack of Jolly Ranchers candy lay just inside the door, and her bedclothes were hanging off the loft. She has got to learn to take care of her things, I thought. She has so much more than I ever had, and she doesn't appreciate it. Jenny, just out of bed, stood in the middle of floor, her flyaway blonde hair unkempt from sleep.

"This is it. You have got to clean this up today. Do you hear me?" I glared at her.

Tears glistened in her eyes. "Okay, Mommy."

I slammed the door as I left the room. I was so tired of this battle. Why couldn't she just do it? I went to the kitchen. The chocolate chip cookies we'd made last night beckoned to me. I ate three. Jerry was at a home maintenance workday with Empty Tomb, a local Christian service agency. I was glad he could help out people who needed leaking roofs patched, but I needed a hug just now.

I sat on the back steps and stared at the bare backyard. Surrounded by the tall grass of early spring, a concrete sidewalk led to the alley with a side run to the detached garage. In Jenny's sandbox, the sun glinted on the new Tonka truck Jerry had found at a garage sale. That'll just rust, I thought. Jenny is never going to learn.

Taking a deep breath, I gathered myself up. Drawing a drink of water at the kitchen sink, I could hear Jenny crying in her room. She's probably not done anything. Picking up a wooden spoon, I marched to her door. Up on her loft, she startled as I opened the door, brandishing the spoon.

"Doggone it, what are you crying about?" I hit the door frame, cracking the spoon.

"I'm crying 'cause you're mad at me." Tears gushed from her big round eyes. She wiped them away.

I stood in the doorway, staring. "Oh. Well, you need to get this place cleaned up, okay?"

"Okay, Mommy."

I went to the kitchen to get the broom. "Here, I'll sweep everything into the middle of the room." I pushed clothes and Jolly Ranchers and colored pencils into a pile. "Now, start picking up the blue things." She clambered down the ladder and picked up a pair of blue jeans. Shutting her door, I sank into the couch.

She cried because I was mad at her. Was that always why she cried? What kind of a mother was I? I was trying as hard as I knew how to give her what she needed. But a child needed more than I had to give. My raging at Jenny grew out of my fear of not fulfilling my responsibilities before God for her. If I didn't train her right, God wouldn't be pleased with me. I'd never thought my parents were pleased with me. Both the sexual abuse and the disinterest conveyed rejection. I wasn't worth much. That fear of rejection showed itself in so many ways.

Because we had no air-conditioning, Jenny and I often spent summer afternoons at the pool. In July of 1979, just after Jenny's fourth birthday, we changed into our swimsuits and gathered our gear to go to the Urbana Park District's pool. A few clouds provided some relief from the sun as we showed our passes at the entrance. We walked through the changing rooms full of noisy excitement and strewn with kid's clothing. We emerged into the bright light, standing for a minute at the top of the hill that led down to the water, letting our eyes adjust. Just as we reached the concrete apron of the pool, a voice sounded from the loudspeakers.

"Our pumps are broken. We need to close. Everyone out of the water."

"Mommy!" Jenny pulled at my hand as I turned away from the water.

"Honey, it's closed. We can't go in." She began to cry. I was already crying. I couldn't help it. I was so hot, and the fans at home weren't enough. To be refused admittance when we had our foot almost in the water just seemed like more than I could bear that day. We trudged up the hill and went home, neither of us saying much. She went out to her sandbox, while I sprawled on the couch.

Ashamed of my overreaction, I'd stopped crying. In my imagination, though, images began to intrude. In my mind's eye, I walked up to the gates of heaven, where Jesus waited for me.

"Ha, ha; fooled you. You're going to hell, after all. Not good enough," he said with a wave of his hand. I shuddered at the thought of the ultimate rejection.

Our next-door neighbor, an older woman, had died the day before. When I imagined her at the gates of heaven, I could think only about what the scene would be when I stood there. Though God's Word said he wouldn't cast out those who came to him, I wasn't so sure. My fear of abandonment ran deep, and her death brought it to the surface. Maybe this whole thing about God loving us was a big joke. He knew the pool was going to be closed. Why didn't he stop us? Why disappoint us like that?

"Oh God, Father, do you really love me? I need you to reveal your love!" I rubbed my red eyes as I got up to get a drink of water.

Many other situations raised questions about God's care for me and my duties toward him. I answered the phone one morning that fall.

"I need you to make a dress for me." It was a new customer—a gruff-voiced woman who spoke abruptly. To my young mother's ear, she sounded old—at least 70, I thought.

"Okay," I said, "Let's make an appointment for your measurements." I reached for my notebook.

"You'll have to come here. I'm in the nursing home."

"Oh." I didn't have a car during the day and I had a four-year-old.

"I have some gingham material, but you'll have to get thread and a zipper and anything else you need. How much will this cost?"

I named my price, focused on what she'd said about needing to get the notions.

"That seems like a lot, but I guess I can scrape it up." She blew her nose. Through the phone, it sounded like a horn.

What if I said yes? Would lots of women in the nursing home want things made? I couldn't be running around town getting things for them. But didn't God want me to help people? Can I say no?

"Well? Cat got your tongue?"

"Uh, no, I'm just thinking." I grimaced. "I don't think I can do this."

"Why not? What's wrong?"

"I don't have a car. People usually come to me, and they get their own notions."

"Oh, you don't want to help out an old lady, is that it?" She hung up.

Was that it? I crawled into bed, pulling the covers over my head. Jenny, thankfully, was down for her nap. I'm not a real Christian. I can't even be nice to old ladies. She wasn't asking that much. I'm such a jerk! *God, what do you want from me? I'm so scared of losing your love if I don't do the right things.*

I yearned for answers. Not just how to respond when I felt taken advantage of, but also how to know what God wanted. And what about those breakdowns? After the second episode, I'd been put on lithium, a psychiatric maintenance medication. The next time I saw my psychiatrist for a medication check, I asked him for an explanation. I wanted to do whatever I could to avoid a recurrence.

His explanations of manic depression (now labeled "bipolar disorder") discouraged me. He said I needed to be on lithium for the rest of my life or I'd have breakdowns every few years. I'd already had two in two years. I was looking for something more psychological. In his office that day, I asked, "What would we talk about if I came in regularly for counseling?" Maybe the answer to that would show me the psychological causes. But all he said was: "Whatever you wanted to talk about."

"So there's not some particular thing that causes manic-depression?"

"No, it's a biochemical illness." He steepled his hands and leaned back in his leather chair.

"Biochemical. So there's nothing I can do."

"Not 'nothing.' You can learn to manage the illness. I'd be glad to help you with that."

But I couldn't afford therapy, anyway. And his answers just frustrated me. I wanted hope.

Because the psychiatrist had no answers for me, I asked God. I wrote my request in my journal, with a date: October 30, 1979. It had been two years since the second crisis. "Help me understand so maybe it won't happen again."

God began to answer the next day. Jerry and I, as was our habit, were lying in bed together, reading before sleep. In the new issue of *Logos Journal* magazine, I saw words that changed my life. A chaplain quoted a schizophrenic woman: "I've always been taught you should be so good before taking the Lord's Supper."

Then he wrote: "Here was her guilt—a core problem in the lives of persons with mental-emotional problems."

In my journal, I wrote:

That hits home. I think that God is going to just throw me away if I don't do tremendous things for him—intercession, drama ministry, some other enormous, demanding activity. God has helped me a lot with free-floating guilt, and I feel pretty close to being healed of such high requirements for acceptance. A growing awareness that God will accept me—that he may not have a demanding work for me to do . . . that he will welcome me with open arms if I'm only able to be faithful to my family—Jerry and Jenny.

As I wrote those words, a warmth I'd never felt before began at the top of my head and flowed through every inch of my body. In one swoop through my being, God's love filled my heart. He was smiling at me. His arms were open as I walked into his embrace. It was the revelation of the Father's love I'd been asking for.

Jerry noticed my deep breathing. "You okay?"

"Never better." I leaned over and kissed him. I could have kissed the whole world. Though excited, I also felt a deep calm. That was new. Excitement usually led to racing thoughts that made it hard to get to sleep. That night, though, I drifted off easily, with a sense of Jesus' arms around me.

The next morning, I picked up my Bible and opened to Jeremiah, where I'd been reading the last few weeks. I'd been making an effort to read the Bible more consistently. The women at Prayer and Share all seemed to set aside a daily quiet time for prayer and Bible study.

Jeremiah rang with God's thundering judgments against his people for their disobedience and rebellion. I knew I was disobedient, too. I didn't know exactly in what way, but there was always more I could be doing. That morning, though, as I began to read in chapter 26, something clicked.

Verse 3 says, "Perhaps they will listen and each will turn from his evil way. Then I will relent and not bring on them the disaster I was planning because of the evil they have done." God wants to change his mind and stop the punishment. I looked around my cozy house. I thought about my good husband. God has given me so much. I wrote in my journal:

> It's taken a long time to have a real sense of God's desire for me—that he has good things for me—that he grieves at my sin; not sadistically rubs his hands together as he looks forward to seeing me in pain as I live out the consequences of sin.

I had not yet realized how my father's seeking pleasure at the expense of my pain had impacted my image of God. What I knew at the moment God revealed his love to me was a joy I'd never felt before. That surface feeling of joy didn't last more than a few weeks, but it settled in my heart. Previous to this revelation, I had only hoped in his love. After this revelation, my roots grabbed hold of the soil of his tender care.

Within a few months, I decided to try to stop taking the lithium. I'd gained twenty pounds, and I felt lethargic much of the time. I discussed it with Jerry and he agreed to let me stop and see what happened. We didn't consult the psychiatrist, knowing he would advise against it because bipolar disorder is a chronic illness. No professional would advise a bipolar patient to discontinue medication. (Frankly, I'm concerned that a patient reading this might follow my example. Please don't! Bipolar does have a strong biochemical component that medication helps.)

My first symptoms of mania had been racing thoughts. Over the next few years after stopping the lithium, I occasionally experienced that feeling of not being able to turn my mind off, especially at night. At those times, Jerry prayed for me, and God always calmed me, enabling sleep. Within ten years, even those initial symptoms subsided.

I believe God miraculously touched my bio-chemistry, at the same time as he challenged me to work through the pain and grief of my childhood. Except for taking trazadone as a sleep aid during menopause, I've taken no psychiatric medications since I stopped lithium in 1979. Am I healed? I think so, but I'm wary, still. I take good care of myself. I get enough sleep, I eat a healthy diet, I keep a manageable schedule, and I have worked hard to fully forgive everyone who's ever hurt me, especially my father.

But I'm getting ahead of my story of forgiving my father and attaching to God. Going off the medication was only a backdrop to those emotional and spiritual battles. I fought to believe God's truths and doubt Satan's lies. Even after the victory of experiencing God's love, I suffered periods of depression. But before that revelation, depression had been the air I breathed.

CHAPTER 11

RECOGNIZING DEPRESSION

Depression begins in loss or void. My whole childhood was devoid of attention, affection, or emotional comfort. When I say that, I feel I'm saying it too harshly. In some ways, my parents were adequate. I had food, shelter, and education. But when I imagine my mother, I see her behind the newspaper. When I see my father, it's the abuse scenes. I felt unwanted, unseen, and used.

When the heroin addicts invited me into their Cadillac, I felt wanted. Starved for attention, I engaged sexually with almost any man. When Jennifer was born, my depression deepened into psychosis. After recovery from those episodes, the depression remained to dodge my daily footsteps. Especially before God revealed his love to me in 1979, I barely rolled out of bed in the morning and couldn't wait to go back to bed. My most substantial verbal prayer in those days was a groaning, "Oh, God," as I opened my eyes each morning. For several years, that was the extent of my prayer life.

In those days, my housekeeping was as minimal as my prayer life. In 1978, I started attending Sunday school classes on marriage and parenting taught by an older woman at UAG. We sat in a circle behind fabric panels blocking out the sight, if not the sound, of the other classes assembled in the church gymnasium. She and her husband had raised four children on the mission field, all of whom served the Lord. In class one day the subject of housekeeping came up.

Someone asked, "How do you keep things picked up?"

"Use an apron with several pockets, so when you walk through the house, you can carry misplaced objects to where they belong." She smiled at the group. We were thirty years younger, at the beginning of our marriages, with young children. Her children had children of their own. "A place for everything and everything in its place."

As we exited the gymnasium, I fell into step with the questioner. "Did that advice help?"

"No. It's not how to clean I need help with, it's desire." She laughed but with chagrin in her voice.

"Yeah, me, too. I can figure out the mechanics. I can't figure out how to make myself do it!" I walked away, wondering if I would ever keep a clean house. As I spoke, three days of dishes were stacked on the counter. I couldn't remember when I'd cleaned the kitchen floor. I did clean the bathroom yesterday, I reminded myself. That wasn't enough, though. Why couldn't I take care of the house? What was wrong with me? I was just lazy.

Entering the sanctuary, I glanced up to the platform at Irene, an older woman who played the organ. She had befriended me, often taking me for a ride in her Volkswagen Beetle to enjoy the green countryside and hear my heart. In her outdated suit, she looked old-fashioned. I needed some old-fashioned comfort just now. Class had reminded me of my laziness. She smiled at me as Jerry and I took our usual seats three rows back in the center right section. Maybe I could talk to her after the service.

When the final strains of the closing song, "And Can It Be," reverberated, I asked Jerry to get Jenny, while I approached Irene. Arranging the dust cloth over the keys, she looked up.

"Hey, how are you?" Her kind smile warmed me.

"Okay, I guess. Do you have any time this afternoon?" I fingered the cloth. It was soft and pliable.

"Do you want to take a ride in the country? That could be arranged." She put her arm around my shoulder. I leaned into her understanding.

When she drove up at 3:00 that afternoon, I was watching at the window. Jerry was glad to be with three-year-old Jenny. They were going to play in the wooden sandbox Jerry had constructed. He had so enjoyed digging in his sandbox when he was little, and he enjoyed it still, with his own little girl.

He squeezed my shoulder before I ran out the door. "I'll pray for you."

We drove out of town on Route 130, but we soon turned off onto farm roads where the corn was waist high on this July day. I began to complain.

"I'm so lazy," I said. I threw up my hands, hoping for disagreement. "Dishes are always piled up; my house is filthy."

"Lazy. That's a harsh word." Irene glanced at me, her face soft. "Maybe you're unmotivated. It's not worth it to you to clean."

"That's true, it's just too hard. I can make myself do it only if the dust is thick, and the floors are sticky."

"See, it just takes the right motivation. You clean when it feels worth it to you."

Motivation. Maybe she was right. *Lazy* wasn't exactly the right word. Unmotivated was changeable; however, getting motivated was still a problem.

At the Tuesday morning Prayer and Share time, soon after the talk with Irene, the topic was prayer. The discussion of vulnerability had taken place a few weeks before.

Great, I thought, as I looked at the study sheet Judy handed around the circle. Another place where I don't measure up. As we sang, "Oh for a Thousand Tongues to Sing," I moaned inwardly. *God, how do I learn to pray? How do I keep my house clean? How do I love Jenny?*

I kept quiet as the other women described their daily quiet times, where they heard God and spent varying lengths of time in prayer. Then Judy addressed me.

"Karen, how's your prayer life?" Like the other women there, she'd prayed for me through my hospitalizations. The softness in her voice disarmed me.

"Uh, not so good, actually." I stared at the floor. Tears began to form.

"Do you pray every day?" Sue, next to me, spoke.

"I moan to him in the morning to help me get out of bed, does that count?"

They laughed. I smiled, glad to get the focus off my inadequacy. But they saw through it.

"You're still having a hard time, aren't you?" Sue put her arm around me. Others smiled with soft eyes.

I leaned into Sue, grateful for their support. The tears came in force then. "I just can't seem to stop screaming at Jennifer, and I can't pray more than 'Oh, God,' and all I want to do is sleep."

"Poor baby." Sue tightened her arm. Though I felt a little embarrassed at being the center of attention, I so appreciated their kindness.

"You're going to be okay. Jenny will be okay. God loves you." The leader spoke from her place across the circle. "Let's continue with the discussion now, and we'll pray especially for you at the end."

After the prayers for self-control that day, I only completely lost control with Jenny once. The depression, though, took much longer to lift. But in that season of support from those women, God exposed many weeds and planted many seeds.

After October 1979, when Father-God revealed the depth of his love for me, my desire to let go of deep unforgiveness toward my father grew. One morning in January of 1980, Jenny was playing in her room, just off the living room. I was sitting in a beanbag chair, flipping through a magazine. Dishes were piled in the sink from last night's dinner. We would go have lunch at Jerry's job site later, out in

Yankee Ridge south of town, where he was wiring a professor's new house.

As I leafed through the magazine, a photo of a little girl holding her father's hand and walking in a field suddenly provoked a flashback. Once again, I shuddered at my father's evil.

"No! I have forgiven my father." Paraphrasing 2 Timothy 4:18, I spoke out loud. "God will deliver me from every evil deed." Instantly, in my mind's eye, I saw God stepping between me and my father. God had delivered me, and he was delivering me. He loved me. I took several deep breaths and spoke more of God's word: "He will be the stability of your times, A wealth of salvation, wisdom, and knowledge . . . ." (Isa 33:6, NASB). "The Lord is my light and my salvation—whom shall I fear?" (Ps 27:1). "For God hath not given us the spirit of fear; but of power, and of love, and of a sound mind" (2 Tim 1:7, KJV).

I'd chosen forgiveness, after God had spoken to me from Matthew 18. But those flashbacks had continued. They came unbidden, at unexpected times, triggered by elements of the abuse. For example, seeing a man look through his bifocals at a certain angle as my father had looked at me always brought the abuse to mind. Seeing a young girl with an older man, whether in the grocery store or in a magazine picture such as the one I was looking at, always sparked bad memories. Sex required great effort and concentration to stay emotionally present with Jerry rather than flashing back to my father's violations.

God, what will stop these images? Just then I remembered what someone had said at a recent Prayer and Share time. "We need to pray to be able to imagine what we believe." In my head, I believed what Philip Yancey said, that God was suffering with us when we suffered, but I needed to be able to imagine Jesus with me as my father violated me in the front seat of the Nash.

God, help me see where you were when I was abused. God had changed my prayer. Previously, I'd been angry: *Where were you?* Now I was willing to listen.

Every day for months after that day, I reminded God that I had to be able to visualize him with me. If I couldn't imagine it, I instinctively understood, his compassion wasn't emotionally real to me.

One morning, waking early, an image flashed through my mind: I'm in the cornfield again, in the front seat of the Nash, with my father. But Jesus is holding both of us with tears running down his cheeks. Shutting my eyes tightly, I gathered the covers around me. I drew my legs to my chest. Though I couldn't hold the image for more than a few seconds that day, I finally saw the reality. Tears wet my face. Jesus knew my pain. He wept with me.

As I continued the daily prayer, the image of Jesus weeping became more and more real. When the intrusive images of the abuse arose, I substituted the image of Jesus with tears rolling down his cheeks, holding us both.

Over the next few months, as I felt less distress over everyday intrusive thoughts, I began to remember more of my childhood. A year later, falling asleep one night, I suddenly recalled a nightmare from childhood. My heart pounded as the memory sharpened.

I was running through the barnyard, near the tool shed, with bullets whizzing by my head. Dead people lay all around me, arms at odd angles, blood pouring from mouths and ears. Thunderclouds threatened overhead. The veins in my neck throbbed as I ran between the barn and the crib, out towards the cornfields. I was nine years old. A rocket exploded just behind me, the acrid smell filling my nose.

I'm going to die, I thought, but I couldn't see who was attacking as I zigzagged through the corpses. I threw myself down between two bloody bodies, breathing as slowly as I could, willing my eyes closed. Blood oozed against my bare arm. Grit lay on my lip, but I dared not wipe it off. An enemy soldier appeared next to the casualties on either side of me, holding his bayonet over his head, ready to puncture any beating hearts.

God, I had that dream over and over, didn't I? I suddenly recalled all those nights, waking in the dark after that dream. I would lie very still in that room I shared with my sister. Slowly, the room's ordinary reality would bring me back to a sense of safety. My dresses hung next to Nancy's on the rod suspended between the walls of the windowed alcove. Next to the clothes, the moonlight illuminated the face of my big doll, tilted on the floor. Past the end of our military surplus bunk bed, the bedroom door was closed. Above me, in the upper bunk, my sister breathed deeply. I was in my own bed, not in a war. Usually, an hour passed before my heart rate slowed enough to sleep again.

As I pondered the meaning of the nightmare, I remembered another one, too. In the second one, I'm in a desert, walking alone. The sun is setting. The only road stretches out before me. Tumbleweeds blow across the path. A coyote howls. Soundlessly, a dark figure grabs my arm. I scream, but my voice emits no sound. The struggle to escape always woke me, too. Sometimes in that dream, I crashed a car instead of a dark figure grabbing me, but I never had a voice to scream for help.

Jesus, what do these dreams mean? Wide awake, the memory of the childhood nightmares fresh, I clasped my hands over my head and thought about them more seriously. In a flash of understanding, I realized they typified my childhood's emotional reality: In great danger, I played dead in order to survive, and I had no voice to scream for help. That's exactly how I felt, but could not feel when I was awake. My dreams told the truth. I was in danger. Emotionally I felt nothing, as if I were dead. The one time I'd tried to speak to my mother of the danger, she didn't listen—I had no voice.

I still didn't have much voice with my parents. I had written them when I became a Christian, many years before, but my father wrote he was "shaking the dust off his feet" toward me because I was a "holy roller." In his reference to Jesus' instruction to the apostles to reject those who reject them, I again felt abandoned. What I thought would be good news to them became another conflict.

In the dreams of early adulthood, I also had no voice. I often dreamed of being molested again, or of Jenny being molested. In a typical nightmare in my twenties, I'd be back on the farm. Inadvertently, I'd put myself in danger, and my father would touch me again. When I suffered in the night from those nightmares, the battles raged the next day against the old abuse images. Slowly, over many years, the daily flashbacks and nightmares decreased.

In May 1982, I dreamed a different dream. This time, alone with my father, I exploded: "You ruined my childhood. You're an evil man. I hate you. You had no right!" I beat on his chest with my fists, screaming and crying. I woke with my tears soaking my pillow.

For the first time, at thirty years old, I raged at my father. But it was only a dream. I still couldn't imagine confronting him in person. I was, however, beginning to understand more. I allowed myself to think about my childhood. Especially provoked by times with Jenny, I remembered the little girl I was.

One summer day, Jenny and I were playing in the sandbox in the backyard. As we dug our feet into the cool sand, an image of Nancy's feet came to mind.

Nancy was standing outside our room, talking over the banister to Mom, on the lower landing. I was three years old. When I noticed Nancy's bare feet, I began to make up a song. "Pink feet, bare feet," I sang, dancing around her.

"Leave me alone." She swatted, missing my arm by an inch.

I ran back into the bedroom and climbed into our double bed. Just as I pulled the covers over my head, I heard Mom. "Don't be so hard on her."

A rare memory of my mother sticking up for me, I thought. And I was making up a song! How did I do that? I wasn't musical. I'd taken piano lessons for a few years in early elementary school, but I wasn't particularly good. How sad. I wish they'd honored that creativity.

Lost in thought, I barely noticed the sand seven-year-old Jenny was packing around my bare feet. Any other time, I might have reprimanded her for getting my feet sandy, but considering my mother's advocacy strengthened me. "Here, you sit down and I'll bury your feet, too."

"Okay!" Jenny settled herself in front of me, happy to really play with me, for once. Usually, if I was in the yard with her, I was reading or sewing a hem while she played alone.

That day, as I remembered my own innocent sweetness squashed, I felt a flash of compassion for my younger self. That self-compassion became the foundation of healing from depression. Over the next few years, as I wrestled with God, grieving the suffering of my childhood, compassion replaced shame. But unbelief, questions about free will, fear, and anger all had to be struggled through before I found true emotional health.

CHAPTER 12

BATTLING UNBELIEF

Peter Kreeft, the Catholic philosopher, says, "Kindness is the desire to relieve another's suffering. Love is the willing of another's good."[3] Fathering, loving a child, is willing the child's good. God uses even the suffering that is inevitable in our fallen world to bring a good end for his children.

Intellectually, I was beginning to grasp some of these things, and the revelation of his love rooted me. On February 4, 1981, I wrote about a progression of trust I'd seen in the journal I'd been keeping since March of 1979. I wrote:

> I've finally gotten a handle on the fact of God's love—that he grieves over sin because he knows it's not our best—any separation from him is not

our best. Therefore he reproves and chastens us and allows trials in our lives to impel us to draw closer to him. Oh, the perspective of God!

I really am righteous in his sight. As I hand him a bag of my sin, he hands me a bag of righteousness. It really is as simple as that! . . . I have learned to trust the faithfulness of God more than my own feelings of panic, fear, or doubt.

A core of unbelief persisted, however. One morning I heard a testimony of God's grace on the radio. A man had run out of gas on a long, lonely stretch of highway, on the side of a hill. Perturbed, he huffed and puffed up the hill. As he reached the top, what he saw took his breath away. A semi-truck had jackknifed across the road. If he'd continued sailing along, his death would have been just over the hill. It brought tears to my eyes at my distrust of God's provision because I so identified with that man.

I often questioned God's involvement when things didn't go my way. Though the oak of God's love was taking root in my desert, it would be many years before I could really rest in its shade.

In the winter of 1981, I learned I needed gallbladder surgery. We had no insurance for me. Jerry's employment with the small electrical business provided insurance for him but would not insure me because of my psychiatric hospitalizations.

I'd finished my degree in sociology, but I had not worked in any job connected with the field. Besides student jobs, I'd only clerked at a fabric store for a few months before Jenny was born, and I'd sewn for a few customers. I began to look for a part-time job that could provide insurance.

When a personnel services job at the university didn't work out, I decided to let it go for a while and see what turned up. One Saturday, I prayed, "Please, let there be just the right part-time job in the *News-Gazette* tomorrow." That was more bold than usual. The next day, I saw a Clerk-Typist III job at the Psychological Clinic on campus. At that time, university jobs were not advertised in the *News-Gazette,* only in the campus paper, so I was surprised to see a campus job in the local paper. But the job required a typing speed of fifty words per minute. I had never had a job that required typing, and I hadn't typed at all since college, eight years before. Because I'd prayed for the right job, I decided to practice, though I nurtured little hope.

In 1978, Urbana Assembly called a new pastor when Dick Foth left to be president of an Assemblies of God Bible college. By 1980, we decided the new pastor's leadership style was too different from Dick's, and we left. We joined Jubilee Assembly, an offshoot of UAG, which met in a large house. At twenty to thirty people, it was little more than a small group. In the half-finished basement of that house, I practiced on the church's electric typewriter every day before the civil service test. Jenny was in morning kindergarten, so I worked alone in that dank basement, hoping that God was answering my prayer.

I failed: forty-nine words per minute. I'd interviewed for the job by then, but a decision had not been made. I scheduled a retake for the next week and prayed.

That Friday night, we were walking through the Sears appliance department when we ran into some old acquaintances. Julian was a professor in the psychology department. Arlene had given us their girls' baby crib for Jenny. They were looking at ceiling fans. Julian had tipped up a box to read the instructions.

"Jerry, just the man I want to see." Julian, balancing the box, shook his hand. Arlene smiled. They were warm, kind people whom we had never before seen in public.

"Oh, yeah, why's that?" Jerry said. We stopped to chat under the circling fans.

"How do I install a ceiling fan without getting shocked?" Julian glanced at the instructions on the side of the box as he spoke.

"Let Arlene do it!" Jerry smiled and we all laughed.

That encounter led to going to their house the next morning for Jerry to install the fan. As we chatted, I mentioned to Julian that I was applying for a job in his department and maybe he could put in a good word for me with Stan, the clinic director.

Having failed the first test, I was anxious as the retake approached. I asked God for a word, which wasn't common for me. The times I'd asked, I'd often been disappointed. The YWAM people I knew, though, often asked God for a Scripture, so I tried it again. Isaiah 66 came to mind. Hoping there was an Isaiah 66, I opened the Bible, found the chapter, and read to verse 9: "Do I bring to the moment of birth and not give delivery?" That's exactly what I felt like—all that typing labor with an uncertain delivery. This time, I felt Father-God's comfort. He would give delivery.

I passed the retake at fifty-four words per minute. Julian put in his good word, and the director hired me, even though I had no clerical experience. Having signed up for insurance, I began the job.

To celebrate my getting the position, Jerry, Jenny, and I feasted on cheesy pizza two weeks later. At 4:00 A.M., I woke in gallbladder pain reminiscent of childbirth, much worse than the first attack that had led to the diagnosis.

"Jerry!" Holding my side, I rolled over and shook him.

"What's up?" Instantly awake, he embraced me.

"Gallbladder."

"The pizza was a mistake."

"Yeah, no kidding. I just started the job. I can't have surgery now." My plan called for a year on the job, accrued vacation, and then surgery.

At 8:00 A.M., Jerry called our physician, who prescribed morphine. I held out with nonprescription pain medications until the afternoon, when I began taking the narcotic. I tried to rest while Jerry fed Jenny, but worries piled through my mind. After they ate, Jerry came in to check on me, sitting on the side of our queen bed, stroking my forehead.

"This pain isn't stopping. What if insurance won't cover surgery? It's a more delicate operation if it's inflamed. What if I lose the job?" My fears tumbled out.

"It'll be okay, Karen. Let's call Bernice—ask her." We went to church with Bernice, and she worked in the university benefits office. He went to make the call. When he returned, he said, "She says it'll pay 100%. Even if you lose your job, it'll pay, because it covers you for thirty days after you leave the job." He smiled.

"Oh. She was sure?" I said, with raised eyebrows.

"Yes, Karen, she was sure."

"Okay."

On the morphine, I slept a few hours. In the morning, after my doctor examined me, he referred me to a surgeon, who admitted me immediately, for surgery on Friday, to give the attack time to run its course. I called Stan to tell him I'd be out of work for a few weeks. I wanted his reassurance the job would be there for me. But he wasn't there, so I left a message.

I lay in the hospital bed, enclosed by the curtain that afforded some privacy from my roommate inside her own curtain. IV morphine finally dulled the pain. The hospital atmosphere seemed familiar, and yet different, from the psychiatric hospitalizations. The antiseptic smell, the padding of the nurses' shoes, the striped curtain were all familiar. But I was different. The pain in my side was real, I was scheduled for an actual procedure, and I knew I was in the hospital. Gratefully, I fell asleep.

When I woke, evening was coming on. I'd dreamt of being pulled apart on a torture rack. Maybe I'm not as different as I thought. I startled as a shadow fell across the curtain.

"Hi there. It's time for your bath." A nurse spoke to my roommate.

Calm down, girl, I said to myself, the shadow was just the nurse. I lay back on the pillow and closed my eyes. When I woke again, it was time for dinner. Jerry was there.

Raising the head of the bed, he helped me sit up.

"How's that?" He pulled the table with the dinner tray across the bed in front of me.

"Thanks." I opened the melamine plate topper. "Turkey and dressing. I'm not very hungry."

"I'll eat it. I had just peanut butter and jelly for supper." He smiled, reaching for it.

"Oh, no. I'll eat it. I'm the one having surgery." I speared a piece of turkey. "I'll choke it down," I teased him back. Though our banter was light, I could see the concern in his eyes. The last time he'd seen me in a hospital bed, I hadn't known who the president was, and I had barely known who he was.

"Did you call anybody to pray?" I scooped up some dressing.

"I called the prayer chain. You'll have thirty people praying tonight." He smiled, smoothing the hair from my forehead.

After dinner, Jerry left to pick up Jenny from a babysitter and put her to bed. Stan called then, alerted by his secretary to my concern about the job. He assured me the job was mine: "You just concentrate on getting better."

I tried to read a *Good Housekeeping* Jerry had brought, but my mind wandered. Jerry was concerned about my mental health; and I was, too. Not only were my dreams terrifying, but my daytime thoughts were strangely disconnected. Not wanting to worry Jerry, I didn't tell him my fears. But I was afraid I might be losing it. I didn't realize how much the morphine was disrupting the normal flow of my thinking. And I worried that Jerry might actually leave if I had another breakdown. I couldn't lose him. I had to hold it together.

I put the magazine on the nightstand and pulled up the covers. I dreamt of dark shapes flowing toward me. When the night hospital noises interrupted my sleep, I woke with a start. In the morning, before I saw my hands lying on the bedclothes, I couldn't quite tell how they were positioned. That disorientation was also a morphine side effect, but I didn't know that until later. Then, it just added to my sense that I was really on the edge.

The fears that assailed me, like endless arrows from an unseen enemy, increased my unease. What if Bernice was wrong about the benefits? What if Stan fired me? How could I be sure? Stan had assured me the job would be there for me. Bernice worked in the office where the university processed claims. She knew the policies.

But the fears kept up. What if they were wrong? What if they didn't mean it? Before I'd gone into the hospital, I'd sensed that God wanted to give me a new, positive experience in the hospital, to help heal the memories of those painful times during the breakdowns, but I didn't realize how hot the battle would be. And what if I couldn't win the battle? I stared at the pale blue curtain that enclosed my bed.

Finally, I said, "God, you have to deal with these fears. I cannot." Just then, I remembered Ezekiel 4. I'd thought God had asked me to read the passage a few weeks ago, but Ezekiel's drama of bearing Israel and Judah's sins had made no sense. I pulled myself up and reached for my Bible on the nightstand. In the fourth chapter, God has asked Ezekiel to make a representation of Jerusalem on a clay tablet. Then he is to erect siege works against it, to demonstrate the siege of Jerusalem. God commands him to bear the sins of Israel and Judah, each for a specified time, by lying on first one side and then the other. While tied down, Ezekiel is to besiege Jerusalem.

I glanced at the IV line attached to my wrist. I could feel my heart beating. My hands felt clammy. Suddenly, I heard God. *Besiege your fears.* Like Ezekiel's chains, the IV tied me down. The fears were assailing me; I needed to besiege them, like Ezekiel besieged Jerusalem.

I closed the Bible. "In the name of Jesus, I will not lose my mind again. God has put me here to heal me!" In my mind's eye, I placed each fear in God's outstretched hand, taking my hands off. As I removed my hand, my heartbeat slowed. I took several deep breaths. God seemed to be smiling. In the hospital previously, I'd seen myself gathered into a ball and thrown away. This time, I saw my fears gathered into Father-God's great heart, dissolving in the vastness of his compassion. Standing firm against the fears—of psychosis, of paying for surgery, of the job security—I felt God's peace.

Why was trust so hard? Just then, an image of the cornfield abuse came to me: the front seat of the Nash—my father's violation. That objectification, like I was a toy to play with. I had trusted him without reservation before that day. After that day, I never trusted him again—except on the turtle-hunt day, and that was sure a mistake! I should have known better than to go with him. Stupid! I can't even trust myself. And I sure can't trust my father. So how can I trust Bernice or Stan to look out for my best interests?

Previously, I had associated the breakdowns with the abuse. The surgery was the first time I connected my trust issues with my father's sin. It was also the first time I so deliberately visualized giving God my fear. My ability to understand myself was growing. I'd seen the depth of distrust in my heart. And, with increasing self-compassion, I felt sad for the little girl who'd not been able to trust her father.

CHAPTER 13

FIGHTING FREE WILL

As I began to feel more self-compassion, I was able to have moments of empathy toward Jenny. And yet my controlling nature continued to lead to many overreactions in the next few years. I particularly remember the time I screamed at her like I had when she was younger, before the women at Prayer and Share prayed for me.

One early spring night, we'd been out grocery shopping. As we brought in the bags, Jerry spoke to eight-year-old Jenny. "Time to do your math." Libby had given us an old school desk. We'd put it in a corner of the living room so we could supervise her homework. Jerry pointed to the desk, where her third-grade math book lay. I'd tried to get her to do her homework right after school, but she'd resisted so much that I'd given up. Then we'd gone to the store when Jerry came home.

Jenny plopped herself sideways in the chair, but made no move to open the book. Jerry put down the grocery sacks on the kitchen butcher block table, new last year for our tenth anniversary. I took off my jacket and hung it in the closet in our bedroom off the living room, feeling the familiar irritation rising. Getting her to do her school work was always a battle. Why couldn't she just do it? Nobody ever had to fight me to get me to do my work when I was her age! What's the matter with her? I took a deep breath. Let Jerry handle it.

Before I knew it, though, I tore out of the bedroom door, ran to Jenny, grabbed her arm, and threw her onto the couch. "What is your problem? Why can't you just do it?" She shrank away from me on the soft, frameless couch and fell to the floor, rolling into a ball, crying. Jerry grabbed my arm.

"Karen, calm down." He led me to the back deck. I dropped into a sling-back chair.

"I know this is hard. I'll pray for you. I'll go talk to her." Jerry patted my shoulder and left.

"God, why such battles?" Wailing, I could barely breathe.

You're angry at me because you can't force Jenny to make the choice you would make.

I leaned forward, as if to listen harder. That's it, isn't it? I thought, as I remembered another fight over homework, three weeks ago. I had run into my bedroom, dropped to my knees by the side of my bed, and cried, "I hate you, God, for giving me a child I can't control." I'd often wondered what "gnashing teeth" meant. That night, I knew. But at the same time, part of me had been glad of the confession. I had hoped confessing that deep hatred of God might give him room to cleanse me. In fact, I had felt more tender toward Jenny since then—until tonight.

"Oh, God, how do I accept free will? I hate that I can't control her. How can I get Jenny to do what's right? And how do I forgive myself for throwing her?" I'd never done that before.

I forgive you.

I wiped my nose on my sleeve. "Is that you, God? You forgive me? I'm such a wicked witch."

Either I accept God's grace here so I could go back and be kind, I thought, or I stay angry at Jenny for resisting and at myself for throwing her. I stared at the gathering darkness outside the screened deck. A robin landed on the grapevines that twined up the screens on three sides. When he saw me, he flew away. Three sparrows twittered on the top step of the outside stairs. "God, if you forgive me, I guess I can forgive myself. Maybe."

But why did I get so angry?

I went back inside, my heart heavy with shame. On the couch, Jerry was holding Jenny. They both looked up at me as I entered. Jerry's face was red, as if he'd been crying. Jenny's face was tear-stained. She turned her face to Jerry's shoulder as I sat down beside them. I touched her shoulder. She looked at me.

"Sweetie, I'm sorry. I shouldn't have gotten so mad. But I don't understand why you can't just do the work. The more you fight, the longer it takes. If you'd just do your homework, you could be done so much sooner." The logic seemed inescapable to me; why couldn't she see that fighting only prolonged the pain?

Jenny, silent, snuggled closer to Jerry. He put his arm around me. His face color was normal now, his features soft. I leaned my head against him. How many times we'd played out this scene.

Why couldn't I deal with this? In some ways, her school work battles had lessened since we'd taken her out of a private Christian school and put her in public school earlier that year. In her new school, the spelling words were easier, the math was half a grade behind, and the reading was more manageable.

A memory of my parents yelling at me about my school work came back. I was late finishing a report for sixth grade English. It must have been ten o'clock, because my parents were already in bed. I was at the desk in the living room that adjoined their room. Through the curtain that separated the room, my father yelled, "Get to bed. Forget about that work."

"I have to finish this. I'll get an F if I don't turn it in tomorrow." I'd just realized I'd begun writing on the back of the first page, which wasn't allowed. The whole paper would have to be rewritten. Crying, I gathered my papers and ran to my room, where I stayed up until midnight to finish the assignment.

Although as students Jenny and I were opposites, my father and I were equals as parents. Neither my yelling nor my father's helped. I wasn't any better a parent than my father had been to me. My heart felt like dead weight.

"Time for dinner, Karen." Jerry's voice interrupted my ruminations. "Why don't you make something while I help Jenny with her homework."

"What? Oh, yeah. In a minute." I didn't know how long we'd sat there, recovering.

He took Jenny to her desk and put her in the seat, pulling up a chair next to her.

"Okay, what's the assignment?" Jerry put his arm around Jenny's shoulders. Her glance at him expressed relief at his intervention.

I can't imagine being a single parent. In the kitchen I flipped on the light. Putting water on to boil, I pulled out a box of spaghetti. Measuring out a big handful, I tried to visualize my father helping me with homework. Of course, I wouldn't have needed it. Besides, though he was always reading, he had finished only eighth grade.

I pulled out some hamburger and crumpled it into a skillet. But my father did not engage with me like that. If he'd offered, would I have let him? Would I have even trusted him to be physically close to me? Except for the turtle-hunting incident, if I had a choice, I'd kept my distance. I opened a can of herbed tomato sauce. But maybe I'd have let him help me with math when I was little, I thought. I had so wanted an attentive father.

I wish I'd had what Jenny has. A familiar jealousy rose in me as I stirred the sauce and checked the spaghetti. That's where some of this anger comes from—that jealousy. I want a father and I'll never have one. Although I didn't like to admit it, jealousy was the word. *Oh God, help us.*

I set the table with the blue and white Corelle plates. I thought of how Jerry always put Jenny to bed. "Put me to sleep," she'd say to him, and they'd go into her room to read and pray. I guess my grandmother read to Henry and me sometimes, but not in my room, sitting by the side of my bed so I could fall asleep, listening to her voice. Certainly my father never entered my room—I'd have been terrified if he had.

"Time for supper, guys." I ladled the spaghetti and sauce onto our plates and put out the garlic toast.

"Can we have chocolate ice cream for dessert, Mommy?" Jenny reached for the green shaker of parmesan cheese.

"Are you done with your homework?" I glanced at Jerry for his confirmation.

"Almost," she said. Jerry nodded his head. He looked relieved at my even tone of voice.

"When you're done."

"Okay. I'll get done quick!"

Later, on the candle-lit deck, amidst a chorus of crickets, we'd eaten ice cream. I went to bed while Jerry settled Jenny.

As I pulled up the light blanket, old memories assaulted me. The feel of my father's hand on my bare bottom. I recalled, too, those nights he raged through the house, furious at Fred or Craig. I cowered in the corner of the kitchen those days, or ran to my room. Suddenly I thought, no wonder I was so scared when he got so angry. He kept shotguns in the house. Were they loaded? Did I know then whether they were loaded? What was he capable of? If he could violate his little girl's trust so calmly, why not kill us all when he raged? I never felt safe in that house—not physically, sexually, or emotionally.

I thought, I don't feel safe now, either, in my own mind. So many fears, like howling wolves. How is Jenny going to get through school? Will she know Jesus? What's her future? Will she ever learn to stop fighting her responsibilities? Am I doing enough for God? What about being a missionary? Will I have another episode of psychosis?

Jerry came into the room then and climbed into bed. "Are you okay?"

"Yeah, I guess so. I wish I didn't get so angry with her."

"I wish you didn't, either." His tone was even, but he'd told me before how upset he got when I was mean to her.

"I know. I was awful, tonight. But I was good with her afterwards, wasn't I?"

"You were, yes. What happened tonight? I've never seen you so mad."

"I know. I'm trying to figure that out."

"Well, let me know when you make sense of it. I'm tired now. Let's get some sleep."

"Okay, sorry." We both knew if he didn't stop me, I'd talk for half an hour. As he fell asleep beside me, I continued to think.

Free will. That's the big issue here. Jenny's free will. My father's free will. God giving us free will. At least, the possibility of choice. I didn't know how it all fit together—God's sovereignty, man's free will—but it sure looked like God had given my father the choice to do evil. And I couldn't make Jenny do what she needed to do.

I closed my eyes to try to sleep. But I jerked my eyes open as I heard: *Your fears about Jenny are sin. You are not trusting me.* The words seemed so clear, I thought I'd see Jesus at the end of my bed.

As my racing pulse slowed, I thought, that's certainly true, isn't it? My anxiety is sin.

God, how do I trust you with Jenny? I'm so afraid. Will she know you? Will she succeed in school? My fearful prayer filled my heart.

You want to control what I don't give you to control.

Yes. You're right. I want to be able to make Jenny do her schoolwork. I don't want her to have a choice. Please help me accept that I cannot control her. Help me recognize the extent of my control. I need your grace to be responsible for what I can do to help Jenny. Amen.

Finally, I fell asleep. In the morning, my first thoughts turned to prayer again. *What do I fear? That you are not there for her? That you are not powerful enough to direct her life? I confess a distrust of your power in her—set me free!*

I could hear Jerry in the kitchen, getting cereal out of the cupboard. I turned over and tried to go back to sleep. He'd feed Jenny breakfast. I had a few more minutes before I needed to see her off to the school bus stop across the street. The change to public school meant freedom from carpooling duties.

But the thoughts of the previous night had brought to a head my battle with God about free will. I was so anxious about Jenny. I'd confessed that, when God showed me the sin in it.

But, God, what about allowing my father to do such evil? How could you stand by? The quote on a bulletin cover tacked to the wall jumped out at me: "I will lead you in the path you should go."

I began to cry. *Why not push us in the right path—just leading us isn't enough! Were you really weeping with us? I can see you in the cornfield with us, but how could you be there and not stop it? Free will costs too much! I've suffered so much—the abuse, the social rejection, the deep depression. How is that worth it?*

I knotted the sheet into my mouth to muffle my sobs. My body shook. I gasped for air. *It's not worth it, do you hear me?* The scream in my head thundered in my skull. The revulsion of the memory of the touch of my father's fingers nearly gagged me.

I dragged through my day. When I lay down again that night, the battle continued to rage. But I was getting tired. I felt like Jacob, wrestling all night with God's angel. Like Jacob, though, I would not let God go until he blessed me. While Jerry put Jenny to bed, I wrestled with the angel and my own anger.

But finally I was at the end of my resistance.

All right, you win. You've got to sort this out for me. As I prayed, I sensed my anger draining away. He has to know what he's doing. He's got to be a good God. There's no sense in following him if he's not.

I remembered a few weeks ago when I'd been sick with stomach flu. I hate to vomit—I'd rather have diarrhea three days than vomit once. That night, though, I kneeled over the toilet bowl and submitted. "You're a good God. No matter what I feel like, no matter what it looks like, you're a good God. Even if I have to do this thing I hate."

That night, saying "yes" over the toilet seemed like a microcosm of the battle with God about free will and suffering. In a world of choice, suffering is always a possibility. We suffer because of our own self-destructive choices. We suffer from the sins of others. And we suffer because of Adam and Eve's first sin. Whether large or small—abuse or vomiting—suffering is built into the system that God has designed. I could either accept that or fight it. I was getting tired of fighting.

Besides, when I took three giant steps back and looked at my life, I was grateful for God's gifts. Jerry was a good man, a good father, and a good husband. Jenny was just a little kid. I expected too much from her. I expected too much from myself. Moms and kids have battles. There's no way around that. I'm supposed to set the boundaries; she's supposed to test them. Just like me and God. He sets the rules. In my anger, I pushed against his boundaries. I had to accept his boundaries, just like Jenny needed to respect the boundaries I set for her. I wanted to stop fighting with him about the world he's made. It's his world, and he's made it a world of choice. Besides, what's the point of fighting God? God, who's given me so much good? I flipped off the light switch on the bedside lamp and was asleep before Jerry came to bed.

In that season of seeing the depth of my heart rebellion and hatred toward God, however, I learned a new prayer. "Lord, I lay myself open before you. Clean me out and fill me up." I prayed that prayer regularly as I moved into a new life phase.

CHAPTER 14

Overcoming Fears

I cannot imagine going back to school. It's been nine years since I graduated. I'm just a housewife." Alone in the house, I fell on my face on the carpeted floor of the living room. The old embedded dirt smelled musty. My tears soaked the fibers as I clenched my fists. "What if I'm wrong about this sense of calling? What if I can't do the work? What if I'm not accepted? Besides, why should I do it? Why put myself through all that work?"

Besides the anxieties about Jennifer's future, I was worried about my own future. In early 1982, after a year of working at the Psychological Clinic, the job I'd gotten when Julian put in a good word for me, I started thinking about an old dream. When I was in college, I'd considered going on to graduate school in counseling. The counselor at Illinois Valley Community College had taken me seriously. I could talk to him about my fears, and he'd helped me see some of my own potential. He had made a difference in my late adolescent world.

That dream seemed far away by this time, though. I could barely parent my child without seriously abusing her. How could I think about doing psychotherapy? I needed therapy; I wasn't a candidate to be a therapist. We should have been in family therapy, and I should have been in individual therapy myself. But we didn't have the money, and besides, I felt too ashamed to describe my behavior to an outsider.

But the idea of being a counselor had begun to take root, though I could hardly imagine it. That day, on the floor, I sobbed and wrestled all morning. Finally, I said to God, "If you want me to be a therapist, you must make it happen." I rose from the floor with little sense of hope, but with a greater sense that he was now responsible, not me.

The next day, at the clinic, I was typing at my desk when one of the professors came into the office, shaking his head over an encounter he'd just had with another professor. I said, "Well, he must have been an egghead in high school. Probably nobody liked him, so he never learned to get along with people."

"Yeah." He pulled out a file from the cabinet behind me and opened it.

I turned my chair around to face him. "He's just treating others the way he's been treated."

With raised eyebrows, he looked up from the file. "You're a clinician!"

"Yes!" My heart leapt as I realized he was right. As if from the corner of my eye, I sensed God in the corner, smiling.

Later that month, visiting a friend in the hospital awaiting surgery, I ran into another friend who'd graduated with a doctorate in social work a few years before. I hadn't seen Barbara in a couple of years. We sat at Loretta's bedside together.

"How are you feeling?" I asked Loretta. Her left fist grasped the bedclothes.

"Scared."

"It's hard to put yourself in the surgeon's hands, isn't it?" I patted her fist. She released the blanket.

"Yeah. What if his hands slip?" Loretta replied with a weak smile.

"I know. It's scary. But we'll be praying for God to steady his hands and give him wisdom. It's at 9:00 in the morning, isn't it?" I patted her shoulder, feeling the heat of her anxiety through the thin hospital gown.

As Barbara and I walked to the elevator, I mentioned I was considering graduate school in social work. She said, "What a good idea. You really should be a counselor. You were very good with Loretta."

"Really, do you think so?" I couldn't see what I'd done.

"Yes." She pressed the elevator down button and faced me. "You empathized with her and directed her toward God's faithfulness."

"Oh, yeah, I guess I did. I just told her what I wanted to hear when I was in her position."

"And that's why you would be a good therapist—you've been through lots of pain—you know what it feels like."

As the elevator door opened, we stepped inside. As I pressed the lobby button, I thought, do I really have what it takes? Did God send Barbara at just this moment?

"Father," I wrote that night, "you are a good God, or I wouldn't trust you with my heart. You know the bruises and brokenness that yet remain. You know what healing I need to be whole and effective as a counselor. Again, I give you my heart, and I give permission for you to do whatever is necessary to heal me and to free me from the fear of rejection. Such freedom I can envision! Oh God, tread tenderly—you know my frame, that I am but dust and fragile. I commit myself to cooperating in this healing as you give me grace and strength."

In the next few months, God strengthened my conviction that I should pursue graduate school. I'd learned some of the language and concepts of therapy from my work at the clinic. The student clinicians wrote opening and closing summaries of their work with clients. Typing them had taught me something about how therapists conceptualized client problems. Conversations with the student psychologists had contributed to my understanding of the process of therapy. Father-God had provided an internship before the internship, though I didn't realize it then. What I knew, at that point, was that I probably could do the schoolwork—the intelligence and core skills were in me.

But it was that old fear of rejection that made my hand tremble in the fall of 1982, as I handed in my application for graduate school to start in January 1983. Not just "Will I get in?" but also, "Will I succeed?" Graduate school and professional life, like nothing else I could imagine, would create situations with high performance anxiety. Would I be able to give my opinions in class? Would the professors like me? How would I know how to help clients?

But line upon line and precept upon precept, God encouraged me. As I prayed daily for healing from fear, courage grew in that first semester. For several years, I'd had a sense that what Jesus said to Peter was also for me: "Simon, Simon, Satan has asked to sift you as wheat. But I have prayed for you, Simon, that your faith may not fail. And when you have turned back, strengthen your brothers" (Luke 22:31–32). The breakdowns had felt like Satan's sifting, and doing therapy would strengthen the brethren.

God also spoke to me in the spring, as I was driving along Interstate 74, returning from taking Jenny to see her Grandma Libby for a week. Along the roadside, new cattails glowed green among old brown stalks, and I heard that still small voice:

> *The new will choke out the old. The old is dead and gone, but the new is alive and vigorous—you don't ever see blooming cattails with last year's stalks. Similarly, the new stuff in your life—the good of the last five years, particularly—will crowd out the old. Indeed, the old stuff is dead—let it die.*

God also encouraged me in many other ways, and the old fears of rejection began to be rooted out. As I prepared to be a therapist, though, that fear would stymie me more than once.

In 1982, we began attending New Covenant Fellowship (NCF), after Jubilee Assembly had dispersed when the pastor left town. By 1984, I was part of the leadership team for one of the three house churches of NCF. These house churches were larger groups, made up of several small groups, which met twice a month.

That summer, the leaders met to pray and plan, and we agreed to tell our stories. In this group of a dozen people that I'd known for two years in various church contexts, I decided to risk telling the whole story. When the night came, I read my prepared statement for about ten minutes to the others gathered in Gary and Shirley's comfortable living room. Sheila and Paul, the leaders, along with others, listened with soft eyes and warm faces. When I finished describing the abuse, the psychoses, and the long depression, they shared their thoughts and impressions.

"She's my daughter and I'm proud to be her Father." That's what Sheila heard God say.

Paul added his impression: "I see a fire inside you, with tongues of flames emanating from you. A beautiful sight. The fire has a purifying effect . . . on you and on others."

Others thanked me for sharing so intimately because it encouraged them as they were working on their own emotional pain while Gary, a psychotherapist, said I'd always understand my clients because I'd felt what they did. I chewed on their words for days afterward. Again, God had provided nourishment.

The class work for the degree took two-and-a-half years of part-time study while I continued to work twenty hours a week at the Psychological Clinic.

Then I needed an internship site—an agency where I'd begin to see clients, under close supervision, for several months. The director agreed to let me intern at the clinic, so I finished the clerical job in August and began an internship in September of 1985.

Because I was changing roles from clerical to professional, I'd determined I'd wear only dresses to accentuate the change. I'd sewn several new ones. My new shared office was across the hall from the clerical office where I'd worked for four years.

The night I saw my first client, feeling competent in a new red and white print dress, I walked across the hall to the waiting room. I'd learned a lot in my classes. We'd done dozens of role-plays of client situations. I thought I was ready. I ushered the young woman into the small office. Dressed in a wrinkled skirt and stretched out cardigan, she slung her large leather bag on the floor as she sank into the chair. I sat in the other chair. I took a deep breath. "How can I help you?"

"I'm having trouble getting out of bed. I missed my 11:00 literature class every day last week. I'm afraid I'm gonna fail it."

"What's your major?"

"Music. I'm a cellist."

"Where are you from?" Oops, that question is too simple.

"Park Forest."

"How long has this been going on—that you can't get up in the morning?" There, that's a better question.

"All last year. That was my freshman year. But it seems worse."

"How's that?"

"I couldn't get up for 8:00 classes last year. This year my earliest is 11:00. I can't make them either."

"How's your mood?" Maybe she'll talk more about that.

"Bad."

"Bad? How so?"

"Just bad."

"Does anything cheer you up?"

"Music does, some. But later, I feel even worse."

"So, music sort of helps but then you feel worse afterwards."

What was that about? She looked so sad. It didn't occur to me it would be so hard to get a client to talk. What am I doing here? Is this all a big mistake, thinking I could do this? I tried to refocus on the client. She was staring at the wall. She hadn't smiled once.

"What else can you tell me about yourself?" I fought my rising panic.

"There's not much to tell. I'm nineteen. I grew up in a normal home. Something must be wrong with me. I didn't have this trouble in high school."

In the rest of the hour, I kept asking questions that she met with minimal answers. At the end of the session, I walked her to the hall outside the waiting room at the top of the stairs, feeling like a complete failure.

"Okay, I'll see you next week." At least she'd rescheduled.

"Okay, bye." Her shoulder drooped under the weight of the bag as she started down the stairs. I was staring after her when a clinical psychology student came out of the waiting room and said good-bye to her client. Connie had been seeing clients for a couple of years and we'd often discussed the therapy process.

We walked to my office on the other side of the stairway. Closing the office door, I turned to face her where she sat in the chair next to my desk. "I can't do this!"

"What do you mean, you can't do this?"

I looked away. I stared at the poster of the Irish countryside on the east wall. I longed to transport myself into its cheerful roads through the green pastures. "Doing therapy is so much different from talking about doing therapy." I sank into the desk chair and looked at Connie. "She hardly talked."

"This is just a first session. You just needed to get to know the person." She smiled.

"I guess I did that a little." I told her what I'd learned. Then I asked, "What was that part about feeling worse after she plays?"

"Maybe the music somehow brings up old pain. Her childhood probably wasn't as normal as she thinks. Remember, most people think they had a normal childhood. Next time, ask her more specific questions about her parents. Like how she felt about them, that sort of thing. And don't forget empathy. Let her know you understand how she feels."

"Oh, yeah. I got so focused on what I should be doing, that I forgot about warmth and kindness." I stood. "Thanks. I hope you'll be here next week, afterward."

"Probably will. You'll be okay. It's a lot to learn." She smiled at me as she left.

I'm glad she thinks I can do this. She doesn't know how hard my heart was beating by the end of that time. I've jumped from little league to the majors in one day.

As I opened the door at home, Jerry called from the bedroom. "How'd it go?"

I stood in the bedroom door. "Scary. I talked to Connie, though. I guess I'll make it." My heart still raced an hour after the session had ended. Later, as I climbed into bed beside a sleeping Jerry, my thoughts drifted to my parents. I'd been thinking lately how often they had assumed I had evil motives as a child. One Sunday morning I'd had a stomachache. I was about nine years old. When I told my father, he stared at me. "I think you just don't want to go to mass."

"No, my stomach hurts." My protests didn't seem to register. He let me stay home that day, but I didn't feel believed.

Telling the truth didn't please them. Getting good grades didn't matter to them. I was afraid of their punishments and had given up getting their approval. They expected obedience, but they didn't give any praise for it. Nothing was good enough for affirming words, and I was always afraid of punishment.

Anxiety felt so familiar to me that I wore it like a mantle. I'd learned in graduate school that we are attracted to what is emotionally familiar, no matter how dysfunctional. Well, I'd sure put myself in an anxiety-producing situation in the internship!

Oh, God. I fell asleep repeating my old cry for help. I began to dream an old dream. It's the farm house of my childhood, but I'm the mother. I've sent Jenny off to school in the old Nash with my father. They left about half an hour earlier than they needed to. As I started to wash the breakfast dishes, horror seized me. "Oh, God. Protect her. I've put her in danger." I fell to the kitchen floor, sobbing, and woke from the exertion.

Immediately, I thought of my client. I feel like my father, don't I? She's in danger with me in that little room alone together. I'm going to hurt her, not help her. *Oh, God. Oh, God. Oh, God.* The streetlight illuminated the old bulletin. Though I couldn't see the text I knew the words by heart: "I will lead you in the path you should go." *I hope you have hold of me, Jesus. I need you to show me the path.* As Jerry breathed deeply beside me, again I fell asleep praying.

I dreamed again. I'm delivering a baby boy. I hadn't realized I was even pregnant. The baby is very tiny—I can hold him in my hand. I look around at the baby's room in the dream. It's crammed with strollers, toys, and dirt. I begin to change the baby's diaper. "This is a lot of work. I had no idea."

When I woke, I thought, well, that's clear, too. The internship, the "baby" is a lot more work than I imagined. So much harder. I stared at the words on the bulletin, readable now in the morning sun. I could hear Jerry in the kitchen, making toast. Why didn't I realize seeing clients would bring up my old pain and fears? Again, I felt my father's hand slipping into my pants. I rolled into a ball, gathering all the blankets around me. Images of the psych ward flashed through my mind. Meals in bed. No laundry to do. I could watch TV all day. No responsibilities. So taken care of.

The next evening, after Jenny went to bed, Jerry and I sat reading the newspaper in the living room. I put down the comics. "I'm afraid this internship is too much for me. I'm a little afraid I might crack up again."

Raising his eyebrows, he put down the front page. "What makes you say that?"

I told him about the dreams. "I'm afraid I'm going to hurt my clients, like my father hurt me." I wiped away a tear with the back of my hand.

"That's a little extreme, isn't it, Karen?" Frowning, he tilted his head. "Aren't you expecting too much from yourself here?"

"I'm just so afraid." I picked up the comics. He wasn't helping.

But he wasn't done. "You're overreacting. If you crack up, it'll be because of your own perfectionism."

I jerked back in my chair, dropping the paper. He had never spoken so bluntly to me. I took a deep breath. "Perfectionism. That's it, isn't it?" I said. "If I can't do therapy perfectly, by the book, it's not good enough. And if it's not good enough, I'm not good enough. It's either or. Perfect or worthless. That can't be right."

I picked up my journal, my face tightening. As I wrote Jerry's response, I saw how my perfectionism grew out of my old sense of worthlessness. I was trying to be perfect so I wouldn't get rejected. Rejection would expose my worthlessness. But trying to be perfect fueled the anxiety. I couldn't be perfect. The real issue was my sense that I had to be the perfect therapist to be acceptable.

Smiling, Jerry turned back to his newspaper. He could see I'd gotten it. And I did. It was as if God himself had spoken. The issue was not my competence, the issue was my perfectionism. Though I continued to struggle for many years with the anxiety that flows from perfectionism, I often remembered God's admonition that Jerry spoke that night. It was the last time I was seriously afraid of another breakdown.

After this clarity about my perfectionism, I sought regular counseling support from Paul, the house church leader, during the rest of that year. As I continued that internship year, I also gained strength from interacting with the other students, who, though I'd been the office manager, accepted me as a professional peer.

One day I even impressed the professors. Some of my internship responsibilities involved case review. The three other clinic assistants and two professors would gather with a student to review the progress of their work. As we were discussing a marital couple one day, the student therapist described the wife's behavior. She often barked orders at her husband, leaving the husband feeling used. The therapist had previously noted the wife was a sexual abuse victim.

"I wonder if, feeling objectified, she treats her husband like an object." I blurted it out without thinking. I knew the feeling, and I knew how it worked in my life. I'd often treated poor Jenny as less than a person because I'd felt so used. I glanced at the two professors.

"Yes, that's a good way to think about it." One of them nodded in my direction.

"That's very astute, Karen." The other one gave me a broad smile. He'd rarely noted my existence before. I beamed back. Maybe I could do this work. Maybe God will use all my pain to heal others. Just maybe, dreams do come true.

REDIRECTING A

After I received my Master of Social Work degree in May of 1986, Jerry, eleven-year-old Jenny, and I set out in our old Volkswagen bus for two weeks of camping in Colorado. As we drove through Kansas, newly planted fields caught my eye. Observing the orderly furrows, I sensed God saying, *You're a planted field. You've been cleared, plowed, and planted.* Though I still felt like a nomad in the desert, his words encouraged me.

After vacation, I applied for a year-long post-graduate internship with the counseling office of the Central Conference of the United Methodist Church. On the wet August morning when I accepted the job, God said, *I am raining on your field.* I felt his reassurance that days of fruitfulness were at hand, te of continuing anxiety. When I didn't do rapy well enough, I expected rejection, and I ejected myself. The healing from perfectionism was proceeding slowly. But God was fathering me, providing the insights I needed.

One September Sunday, we were returning from Libby and Ed's in a new-to-us used Honda Accord. In contrast to the cold Volkswagen van, I was enjoying the warmth of a functional heater. As usual, Jerry was driving, and Jenny was reading a book in the back seat.

I often spent travel time thinking through my own emotional progress. We were approaching the bridge over I-74 at Mansfield, when a question popped into my mind: Why don't I get angry, except at Jenny? Immediately, the insight came: You're afraid to direct your anger at the proper target because they'll get angry back, and you'll feel rejected. That rejection triggers the deep rejection from your father.

Oh, there's a thought. I stared out the window as we approached I-57. As we passed over the bridge, an orange semi-truck whizzed under us. Fear of being abandoned and rejected lies underneath so much, I thought. *Jesus, you're my counselor. How angry am I? Show me.*

As a therapist, I'd learned that anger is a second-ary emotion. We get angry in response to fear or pain. I easily felt hurt and often expressed that hurt to Jerry, but I almost never expressed anger to him or anyone else. Like that time I fell off the corn crib—and, certainly, following the abuse. I must have been angry, but all I remember is despair. Even early on, I didn't get angry.

One morning a few weeks later while I was lying in bed semi-awake, images of two different parts of myself flitted through my mind. A bedraggled four-year-old self, crouched in the corner of my childhood room, snuggled against my big dolly. Outside the door, an angry twelve-year-old self flailed at God as he held me off with his hand on my head. With clients, I often conceptualized emotional trauma by assigning an age and an emotion to different parts of the self. Suddenly, I saw my own traumas in that framework.

There's the anger. She's twelve years old, and she's mad at God because she couldn't get away from her father in the cornfield. After my father's violation, I'd scrunched against the car door. But he had made that protective instinct dangerous: "I'll do it again if you don't come sit on my lap."

I heard Jerry opening Jenny's door to get her up for school, but it barely registered. The morning light illuminated my beige Singer sewing machine that I'd carried with me when I left the farm. More old memories flooded back. That basement abuse.

I haven't thought of that one for years. I was eight years old then. Still too little to jump off that four foot ledge. I was as imprisoned on that ledge as if I'd been put in a cage meant for an animal. I shuddered.

And at four, in the cornfield. He exerted absolute power in a crazy-making way. My whole body tensed as I reimagined that cornfield scene. I had had no way to escape that double bind. If I didn't trust him and get back on his lap, he would violate me again. But I had no guarantee he wouldn't pull my pants down again anyway.

Such evil had never crossed my mind. Evil came up and slapped me scared, and I've been expecting it ever since. No wonder I always imagine the worst. I wasn't safe with my father. How could he violate me like that? He's still not safe. In our rare visits, his first words were usually an inappropriate comment about my body. I would sue him for harassment if he were my boss.

Where would I ever be safe? My heart felt hollow, my limbs weak, my stomach leaden. I rolled over into a fetal position, gathering the blanket around me. *Why, God? Where were you?* I ground my teeth as my old questions reared their heads. I thought I was done with anger at God. But this was new. Mixed in with anger at God's seeming impotence was a flush of anger at my father. But that anger was elusive.

Only in my dreams had I raged at my father. He was still too powerful. Though he was an old man, he could still hurt me.

We spent Thanksgiving of 1986 with Libby and Ed in Streator. Wanting to access that elusive anger, I set off alone on Friday to go back to the cornfield, knowing my parents were gone to New Mexico for the winter. Just outside town, a new subdivision of brick houses made the old town look prosperous. But on Main Street, the houses hadn't changed since the fifties. A new Casey's convenience store with gas pumps anchored the intersection near the shuttered Chevrolet dealership. Down the street, the white clapboard Presbyterian Church still stood. Had I ever set foot in that church? Though situated only a few blocks from the Catholic Church where I'd grown up in incense and guilt, the Presbyterian Church might as well have been on the dark side of the moon. Catholicism was the church that Jesus had founded. Protestant denominations were founded by ordinary men. That's what I'd been taught.

Though I'd ridden past the outside of that building every week for seventeen years, I'd never set foot in that or any Protestant church in Halesburg. Would growing up Protestant have given me a better grasp of God? I didn't hear a gospel of forgiveness in the Catholic Church. God was as hard-edged as Father Wright, who ran the parish with his iron fist.

God was to be obeyed and feared. Love didn't enter into it. I didn't hear John 3:16–17 until I was an adult. That God was a Father who loved me and, in Jesus, absorbed my punishment, still seemed way too good to be true. Did my classmates who grew up Presbyterian and Methodist hear the gospel as children? Was the good news preached, but I just misunderstood? Or was it Father Wright's failure to grasp the depth of God's compassion? Who knows? I just wish I'd known God's hand in mine sooner.

I slowed down, examining the familiar houses as I approached downtown. They just looked older. The business district looked the same. A block north, one new brick house stood out among the dilapidated houses around it. When I got to the country, I sped past the family farm, up to the intersection where I'd unknowingly turned the corner toward evil. Even after thirty years, the road was still gravel. I crossed the creek and stopped at the entrance to the field, now full of corn stubble.

Right there. That's where it happened. I imagined the old Nash, with its smell of my father's Prince Albert tobacco.

At the clinic last year, a graduate student had given a presentation on body shame. She talked about the common American feminine sense of "something's wrong with my body." No one is happy with how she looks. Shame. I had wrestled with shame not just about my body but about my whole self. On the side of the gravel road, I sat in the car, running the engine to keep warm. As I stared at the corn stalks, that shame rose up in me. Something is irremediably wrong with me. What was wrong with me that my father thought he could do that to me? How could he?

An old Ford truck rumbled by, the man at the wheel raising a finger in the manner of country people. I acknowledged him with a glance but didn't recognize him. So many new people around. I was glad he wouldn't recognize me.

My chest tightened, and the familiar lead weight tugged at my stomach. I was here to touch the anger; not the shame. It happened right here! Where's the anger? I felt as depleted as the winter corn stubble that surrounded me. What's the use? Anger wasn't allowed. My father was the only one allowed to get angry in the family. He could flip into a rage, stomping around the house, bellowing anything he wanted.

Not only was he allowed anger; he liked making others angry. Two months earlier, we had visited them before they left for New Mexico. On Nancy and Joe's enclosed porch, we'd been talking about Mom and Dad's recent Alaska trip. Mom had been complaining. "I wanted to stay longer, but Dad was ready to go. I was mad as a hornet," she said, throwing up her hands.

"Yeah, I really got a rise out of her," my father had said. I glanced at him. He was grinning. Even in the retelling, he was enjoying her anger.

He's a sadist, I'd thought, with a mix of surprise and clarity. Surprise, because I'd never labeled his pleasure in "getting a rise" as sadism. Clarity, because it explained so much. If he enjoyed my anger, why should I give him the pleasure? Instinctively, I must have known that, even as a child. No wonder I'd stuffed my anger. And no wonder I punished myself so much now. Raised by someone who enjoyed inflicting pain, I learned to enjoy pain.

That seemed a little extreme. I wasn't into any kinky sexual behaviors. But then I thought of the couple I'd been working with in therapy. He wanted more sex from her. She wanted more understanding from him. He felt rejected; she felt rejected. I'd tried all the techniques I knew to get them to move toward each other. Nothing was working with them. They were at an impasse. In the back of my mind an endless tape ran: If you were a better therapist, they'd be communicating. The roar of that self-talk hurt my ears.

I stared at the brown field, my insides leaden with shame, remembering those insights about my father's sadism and my masochism. That abuse objectified me. If I'm an object, like a toy, I shouldn't have feelings. Toys just get played with and discarded. Something's wrong with me if I have feelings. All the time I lived here, I felt embarrassed to be a human being.

I couldn't see the house through the trees that lined the creek, but the bathroom, the kitchen, and my old bedroom were as familiar to me as my bathroom, kitchen, and bedroom in Urbana. Even though I knew my parents weren't there, I felt the oppression I always felt at the farm. With a momentary shudder, I put the car in gear.

I left that day with new and deeper awareness of my shame, but no new experience of anger. Mostly I was numb, as if I were in a limbo between the sadness and anger stages of grief. I'd cried and cried, for years. That day, few tears were left, and yet I couldn't touch the anger, either. I'd seen a twelve-year-old angry self, but I hadn't experienced her yet. I was suspended between the four-year-old and the twelve-year-old.

Within a few days, however, the angry twelve-year-old expressed herself. From the beginning of our marriage, our sex life had been a source of conflict. Jerry tried to be patient, but he often reminded me, "You're the only one I can have sex with. If you want to talk theology with someone, you can have breakfast with Paul. I can't go have sex with anybody else." I understood his logic, but I didn't feel he understood how hard I tried to give myself sexually, in spite of the continuing mental images of the abuse that came up when he touched me. "No" didn't ever feel like an okay response to his advances.

I was beginning to feel too controlled, and one night that fall when he began to touch me, I said, "Not tonight, okay?" When he rolled over without a word, I turned my back to him. My heart was pounding. If I can't say "no," how can I say "yes"? I feel like a prostitute.

I uncharacteristically stayed angry for three days, barely talking to him. He spent most of the next three evenings in the detached garage. The fourth night, at the kitchen sink washing dishes after an uncomfortable dinner, I watched him through the window as he walked away from me. I thought, am I so angry I don't want to resolve this? I dried my hands and walked out to the garage.

"Can we talk?" I wrung the dishtowel I'd carried with me.

He glanced up at me from the workbench where he was building a birdhouse. "If you want to."

"I don't want to be mad at you. We keep coming up against this sex thing. I have to be able to say 'no,' do you see that?" Palms up, I shook my hands.

"Yes, I do." He looked at me. "Do you see I want to make love with you?"

"Yes. I want to make love with you, too. I am working as hard as I can on being available to you. I don't think you have any idea how much sex feels like abuse."

"No, I know I don't." He stared at me for a moment before his face softened. "I'm so sorry. Sorry for you, sorry for us." He reached for me and I stepped into his embrace. We held each other and cried. My father's sin penetrated not just my heart, but the heart of our marriage.

Father-God seemed to wrap his arms around us as we wept together. After what felt like a year, I said, "I'll be waiting for you."

"I'll be there in an hour or so. I want to finish the roof on the birdhouse." Through our tears, we smiled at each other.

As I walked back to the kitchen, I thought: I am that angry at my father. I really don't want to resolve it with him. If my father had not violated me, my sex life, indeed, my whole life would be vastly different.

After that day, I began to dig deeper into those old memories because I knew long-term anger would destroy me. Ephesians 4:26–27, about not giving the devil a foothold in your anger, had taught me that. I was beginning to grasp how Satan planted his weeds. The shame I'd felt so clearly at the cornfield at Thanksgiving was Satan's lie: "Something's wrong with you, that's why you were abused. If you were perfect, you wouldn't have been abused."

If God had more healing and growth to work into my heart, I wanted it. I needed a deeper healing of Satan's shame. And somehow, I needed to resolve the rage at my father. That anger was a thicket of weeds in my heart. If I let them, those weeds of shame and anger would choke out God's seed of self-compassion. I wanted to destroy Satan's lies before they destroyed me.

CHAPTER 16

EXPOSING MY HEART

What should I tell that new client from last week who was complaining about his frigid wife? I chewed my lip as I drove across town on my way to the Methodist pastoral care agency. The familiar anxiety revved up like a motor in my midsection. I'd been seeing clients now for a year and a half, but the anxiety still dodged every session.

In my counseling with Paul during the internship last year, we'd not dug into the old abuse issues. But we continued in house church together. In November of 1986, after a worship time in house church, he sensed God had given him a word for me: "I want to touch that intensity with joy." I hoped it was God. I longed for a joy that endured.

After a particularly anxiety-ridden day, in early December, I set up a counseling appointment with him. As I described the cornfield abuse in some detail, he helped me realize just how shattering that first abuse had been. After that session, I wrote in my journal:

> I learned something that has had a fundamental effect in me from that first incident. My childish joy in being alive was shattered by evil of such magnitude that I did not know existed. And I have never regained the joy. I came back from the trip to the store with my father a shattered child, and I have never been able to rebuild the core of joy that I had before that intrusion of evil.

> I tend toward depression, I focus more on negatives than positives, I struggle with all kinds of evil. Though I have made progress in many areas of struggle, it always feels very desperate and despairing when I begin a process.

> I could go back through my writings for the past ten years and see incident after incident where I have struggled desperately not to expect evil. I learned, in a very powerful way, that reality is evil and that hope and joy are illusory.

> I expected failure and, therefore, rejection. My anxiety fed on that expectation. But God, having

exposed the root of anxiety, began to heal it. When I wrote that journal entry, I also wrote my imagery of how Jesus would have treated me if he'd taken me to the cornfield that day:

> If Jesus had taken me for a ride to the store and out into the field that day, he would have shown me the corn and how it was ready to pick. We would have enjoyed the crisp fall air and walked over to the spring for a drink of fresh water.
>
> He would have held my hand, gently but firmly, as we walked. He would have explained how corn grows, and we would have imagined together what gift I might get for my birthday next week, since the crop was good and prices were high. And joy and hope and faith and love would have been my heritage.

During graduate school, I'd gotten close to Bonnie, an old friend of Kathy, the woman I'd gone to Kansas City with in 1977. Bonnie was an energetic, petite woman, who was also on campus getting a doctorate in sociology. We often ate lunch together. Her calmness calmed me. A few days before Christmas, I was telling her about the session with Paul and also about what he'd said in house church about God "touching my intensity with joy." We were in the basement of the University YMCA eating salads.

Bonnie stopped her fork of spinach halfway to her mouth. "That's it!"

"That's what?" I stared at her.

"That's what I've been feeling from God for you for the past two years!" She went on to explain that she didn't get words from the Lord, but she sometimes had feelings that she knew were from him.

I leaned back in the chair, awed by God's personal word. I knew I was intense. Intensity was required to get through all the emotional work. But that focus wore on me. The hope of joy was an amaryllis in the desert.

Wanting to give God space to work in the lies Satan had planted in the abuse, I asked Bonnie and Paul if they would pray with me, after the holidays, for healing of those memories.

We met in my living room one afternoon in January of 1987. I sat on the navy loveseat. Paul pulled up the boxy upholstered chair, while Bonnie sat beside me.

"How shall we do this?" I'd never tried to do this inner healing kind of prayer, and felt nervous.

Paul leaned forward and took my hand, while Bonnie grasped my other hand. "Let's just start asking God to show us how to pray." He smiled.

I took a deep breath and closed my eyes.

After a short silence, he prayed. "Father, we want you to affirm Karen today. Let's start at the beginning. Take her back to her conception."

I immediately sensed myself in a large room, where the Holy Spirit filled every corner. Then I saw a sperm penetrating an egg—my beginning. Both egg and sperm glowed. *I wanted you. That egg and that sperm was the only way. You were worth the risk of giving you to those parents.* God's words were almost audible.

"Father, you wanted me. Please help me want my life as much as you do. You know how much it feels life has not been worth the pain." Releasing Bonnie's hand, I wiped my eyes with the back of my hand.

She shifted beside me. "God, bring joy to Karen's life. There's been so much pain."

"God, it's not worth it. Life is too hard." I sobbed.

"Help Karen hold joy and pain together. Life is both—not either/or." Paul squeezed my hand as he spoke.

I grabbed a tissue from the box I'd set next to us on the couch and blew my nose. "Yes, Lord. M. Scott Peck says, if we question the pain, we don't 'know enough of the joy.'[4] That's true. I don't know the joy. Anxiety obliterates it."

"Take some deep breaths, Karen. Let's just listen for his voice." Paul smoothed his brown hair across his forehead and leaned back. I inhaled as Bonnie and I rested against the loveseat back. I imbibed their kindness in each lungful of air.

"Can I really do therapy? Do I have what it takes? I'm just so anxious when I'm seeing clients, especially before a session."

Paul looked at me. "As soon as you try to quiet yourself, the self-doubt is there, isn't it?"

"Yeah." I stared at the wood grain in the cherry armoire across the room.

Bonnie put her arm around my shoulder. "It's scary, isn't it?"

"And those fears have always been there. I'm never good enough."

Paul leaned forward. "Like there's a sadistic spirit hovering, keeping you off balance." We didn't often speak of evil spirits.

"Yes. You know my father's sadism. Maybe that spirit gained influence when he abused me."

"Let's pray against it." He took my hand again. "Father, in the name of Jesus, we take authority over this sadistic spirit. Karen belongs to Jesus. Satan has no authority in her."

I nodded. "Please, God, Set me free."

Bonnie squeezed my shoulder. "Yes, Lord. You made her for yourself, not for the enemy."

We wrapped up the prayer, then, agreeing we had heard from God.

"Thanks so much." I felt a bit lighter as they left. In the kitchen, I drank a glass of water. Usually I preferred 7UP, but the ice water tasted good today, like God's own nourishment.

That egg, that sperm. I was worth the pain. Not just to me, but to him. God knew my father. God foresaw the pain. I stood at the kitchen window, staring at the frigid backyard. Last night's snow had whitened the brown grass. The piles of junk near the garage looked like flocked sculpture.

Though I felt stronger emotionally that winter, my back began to hurt, including sciatic pain down my leg, which began to interfere with doing psychotherapy, with its hours of sitting. The powerful time of inner healing strengthened my faith to ask for a physical healing.

One day as I prayed for my back, I had an image of lying on my stomach, with three members of a prayer team from NCF touching my lower back, my knees, and my ankles. A week later, I asked them to recreate that vision and God healed my back. I rose the next morning, pain free. In the following Sunday service, I testified to the healing.

However, within three weeks, much of the pain returned. I was angry, frustrated, and disappointed. In that state of mind, I determined to meet with God. Setting aside a morning, eating nothing, I drove to Glen Forest Preserve, about thirty miles away. It was March 25, 1987.

I stopped the old Honda near a bubbling brook. Last summer, Jerry and I had played in that stream. The sun shone on early tufts of grass along the side of the water. A cardinal swooped by on the other side of the little creek. The trees swayed in the spring wind. I pulled on a sweatshirt and picked up my journal. Unmindful of my good jeans, I sat on a large stone and stared at the water. I hugged myself. Still a little cool in east central Illinois in March. I opened my notebook and wrote:

"God, what is going on? Why did you heal my back for only three weeks? Yeah, it's not as bad as it was." Crying, I wiped my nose on my sleeve. I continued writing: "You have all the power here. Why did you take the healing away? Why do it at all if you meant to take it away?" I closed the notebook.

My father used to take things away from me. Sometimes at supper, I'd fill a plate for myself. If I walked by my father with it, he'd ask me for it. Just as I was salivating at the smell of fried chicken or bean soup, he'd ask me to give it up. And of course he took my innocence that day in the cornfield.

I spoke aloud: "God, you are not like my father." I stared at the gray trees across the creek. The cold wind stung my cheeks. "But it sure feels like you are. Show me! I want to give up this anger. But it looks like you use power whimsically! You create pain, and you heal pain. I don't understand."

I opened the book again and wrote: "Capricious. That's how it feels. But that's my father, not you.

Transference. I still expect you to act like my father." My hands felt numb. I climbed in the car to get out of the wind. After rubbing my hands to warm them, I continued to write: "Intense hostility toward Dad for years and years is part of my character." I put down the notebook and I leaned against the seat back.

I spoke out loud. "Yes. I've been angry with him forever. In fact, I hate him." I leaned my forehead against the steering wheel. I'd never acknowledged hatred before. I'd dreamed it. But I'd never said it.

And God has the same kind of power my father had. And like my father—he'll hurt me. It's only a matter of time.

Yes, that is what it feels like.

But that cannot be right.

I picked up the notebook again and wrote: "God, you are not capricious. My father is capricious. You use your power in the service of your love, always. No matter how I feel, no matter what it looks like, you are a good God, and you do only good. Break the bondage. How small my faith is. I want to trust you."

I drove back to Urbana with more awareness of how much I expected God to act like my father and a new determination to sort out those lies. Within a week, my back was well again. I've not had sciatic pain since.

In June 1987, we attended a family wedding in La Salle. At the reception, during the dancing, Jerry, Jenny, and I sat at the end of one of the long rows of white paper–covered tables. Several of my siblings were chatting at another table. Some of their children danced with each other.

My sister, on her way from the restroom, stopped at our table. "How are you guys? I didn't get a chance to say 'hi' at the church."

"We're good. How are you?"

"We're good, too." She moved on towards the food line now forming along the side of the hall.

"I never know what to say," I said to Jerry.

"What is there to eat?" Jenny asked. It was 2:00. We'd not eaten since we'd left Streator that morning, where we'd stayed overnight.

"Yeah, I know what you mean," Jerry said to me. He took Jenny's hand. "Let's go see."

"I'll come, too." I glanced at the dancers, now filling the floor, as we edged around the tables to the wall. The bride and groom, surrounded by friends, danced as if they'd practiced all their lives. Stepping into line, I could smell the Brut cologne of the man in front of me, talking to his companion, her blonde curls sprayed in place.

My sister was several places ahead of us in line. On the far edge of the dance floor, cousins greeted each other. Unmindful of their good clothes, children chased each other under the tables and through the dancers. At a table across the room, my parents were talking to the groom's parents.

They may as well be strangers. I watched Mom and Dad as they laughed and got up to get in the food line. Why try to talk to them? What is there to say them?

I took Jerry's hand and put my other hand on Jenny's shoulder. *Thank you, Jesus; I have a family.* Tears moistened my eyes. *Thank you for Libby and Ed. But I'm supposed to have this family—this big family.* I wiped my eyes. It's just never going to happen, is it? I'm not ever going to get what I want. I wish, just once, my father could say he was proud of me. And does he have any idea what hell I've gone through? Does he care? Why did I even come today?

"I need to go to the bathroom," I said. "You guys get me something to eat, okay?"

Jerry glanced at me. His eyes softened, seeing my red face. Pushing my way through the empty chairs, I found the restroom where my sister had emerged earlier. A stranger was patting her cheeks with powder as I opened the door. Averting my eyes, I opened a stall, closed the door, and stood at an emotional door that had opened before me. Thirty-five years old. The old weight pressed against my chest. With a deep breath, I told myself the truth: I will not ever have the father I want.

Unrolling a length of toilet paper, I blew my nose. The bathroom was empty as I splashed water on my face.

Reapplying lipstick, I smiled at myself in the mirror. *God has given you a new family, girl. Dick Foth at UAG has fathered you. You have dozens of brothers and sisters at NCF. And you have Jerry and Jenny.*

Then, in my spirit, God reminded me: *And I am, myself, your Father.*

Yes. I took another deep breath and stared at my face in the mirror. My red eyes had cleared. When I'd prayed for the baptism of the Holy Spirit in 1972, with the leader of a prayer meeting I attended, he had prophesied: "I am your Father, I am your Father, I am your Father." That was fifteen years ago.

"Yes, Lord," I whispered. "I am your child, you are my Father. You are a good Father, and you have provided a big family. Thank you." I rubbed a dab of lavender lotion on my hands from a counter dispenser and opened the door to find Jerry and Jenny.

A weight lifted that day as I gave up the desire to get attention and affirmation from my family, especially my father. I traded my natural father for my spiritual Father. Henceforth, God was my Dad. I began to call him "Papa." My father had despoiled "Daddy."

In June 1987, as I walked through Plaza Frontenac in St. Louis, Papa-God continued his fathering. Jerry and Jenny wanted to move faster through the ritzy mall, so I set off by myself. After being a size sixteen for several years before graduate school, I'd lost twenty pounds in 1983. At the campground that morning I'd felt good as I put on the sleeveless eyelet top I'd sewn and size twelve jeans.

I loved walking through nice shops, feeling the elegant fabrics. Sometimes I got ideas of garments to sew for myself or Jenny. Jerry often told the story of how I'd seen a drawing of a little girl's dress in the newspaper one Easter and, based on no more than that sketch, made a dress for Jenny.

I ambled toward Saks, passing two women in suits. A woman in a silk dress strode into Talbots. I browsed through Saks' misses department. A saleswoman looked pointedly at my peasant blouse. "Are you looking for something special?"

"Uh, no, I'm just browsing." I moved away and soon left.

Near the center of the shops, at Godiva, a man in linen pants was paying for a chocolate-dipped strawberry that cost more than our three peanut butter and jelly lunch sandwiches. He glanced in my direction.

He's probably thinking, what a country bumpkin! What's she think she's doing here?

I ducked into the next store. Even in the back of the shop, the sale items were twice what I could pay. What am I doing here? Finding the nearest mall exit, I rushed outside. The sky had clouded over, though the heat had not broken. After sweating halfway around the building, I finally found our Volkswagen bus. I climbed in to lie on the mattress. Why did I think I looked good in this outfit? I'm just an abused little girl. I'll never wear silk. My faithful Father-God had exposed another layer of shame.

CHAPTER 17

Papa, Deliver Me!

W e'll sell some next Saturday. People just need to get used to us being here," I said to Jerry. We were packing up our pottery at the Urbana Farmer's Market in July 1987, having sold nothing.

"I don't think so. They're buying food, not art." Jerry threw down the folding table, snapping its legs shut.

After selling his pottery equipment to pay for my second hospitalization in 1977, Jerry had, earlier that year, purchased a new wheel and kiln. In our first years together, he'd thrown stoneware planters, but after getting the new equipment he learned raku pottery, with its exciting process of pulling the hot pot out of the kiln and plunging it into sawdust and water.

"Oh, Sweetie. It'll be okay," I said. On the following Thursday, though, my mood was different. As I opened my eyes in the morning, I felt a familiar weight in my chest. An image of sitting behind the table with the pots at the market last week flitted through my mind. That's it. I'm as frustrated as Jerry is. I just don't own it until four days later. What is wrong with you? You're a therapist and you're not in touch with your feelings. You hypocrite!

I rolled over. Jerry was already up. Breakfast noises, along with Jerry and Jenny's soft voices, wafted through the slatted doors of our bedroom.

I always think Jerry is out of touch with his feelings. But he knew his feelings last week. *Jesus, only you can set me free. I'm as angry as Jerry. I just learned to stuff my feelings because, growing up, nobody cared about them. Deal with me, Jesus.*

I am so tired. Will I ever get past all this leftover garbage from that abuse? I clenched the sheet, pulling it up to my neck. My heart pulsed under my hands. *Jesus, here's a feeling for you: I still hate my father. I hate him, I hate him, I hate him.* Still clenching the sheet, I pushed my fist against my mouth. I'd kill him if I could get away with it. And I hate myself for hating him. I raised myself against the pillow. My chest rose and fell as I consciously slowed my breathing. Releasing the sheet, I lifted my hands and prayed aloud: "I am powerless. If you don't deliver me, I will hate him to my grave."

I picked up my journal. In big letters, I wrote: "God, I don't want to 'manage' this stuff! I want to be delivered!!! Surely you've worked on this stuff this year to heal me!!!"

The next day, I met with Paul and another man and woman to brainstorm about pastoral care issues at NCF. After our discussions, sitting around Paul's oak kitchen table, we usually prayed for each other. When my turn came that day, I said, "I feel so angry I don't even know what about. It's my father, it's me, it's life." They knew my history with my father. We bowed our heads. The other woman put her hand on mine.

"Father, bring your comfort. You know the cry of Karen's heart," she prayed.

After several more brief prayers, the other man spoke. "I keep hearing 'relax, I'm the judge.'"

I lifted my head. "That hits home. I'm always judging myself and thinking I have to meet the standards all by myself. You know I hate my father. I confessed that last time we met. Then I'm angry at myself, can't forgive myself for hating him. Aaah!"

"God forgives the hatred. He's on your side. And he has to help you let it go." From across the table, Paul smiled at me.

"I long to live a relaxed life, but it feels like I'm setting myself up for abuse if I let down my guard. What if God really is just like my father?"

Paul leaned forward, emphasizing each word as he spoke. "God is not an abuser."

"Part of me knows that. I've known he loves me since 1979 when I prayed for that revelation. But I have to relax and trust that love. No matter what happens."

"Yes, you've got it in your head. And you can trust God to root it in your heart," Paul said. Their hugs as we parted comforted me.

After the internship working with Methodist pastors, I began to work in a small group practice, The Communication Center, in August of 1987. The group's director, Elaine, knew my supervisor at the Methodist agency, and she had readily invited me to join the group of therapists who shared space and administrative support.

By early October, I was beginning to build a practice. It was close to home, I liked my coworkers, and the financial arrangement allowed me to offer clients a sliding scale. I looked forward to working there a long time. Though I had prayed for a part-time place to see clients, and God had provided, it seemed too good to be true.

In my journal, I wrote: "There's still about 20% of me that fears that this One on whom I depend for wisdom and stability and knowledge may suddenly turn evil—just as my father did. The joy, at this point, is that 80% of me is quite clear that the experience of dependence that this One has drawn me into is precisely the normal Christian life—filled with joy and hope and faith and love!"

But then, after only three months, one morning Elaine summoned me to her office. "I'm dissolving the group."

I stared at her. Job's words echoed in my mind: The Lord gives, and the Lord takes away. "Okay," I said. "When?"

"In three months."

And the 80% of me who trusted God held. I prayed that night, with tears. "I don't understand, but you are a good God. You know what you are doing. I trust you." I sensed his pleasure.

In the morning, I drove the back roads east of town, through the harvested corn. I clenched the steering wheel. "God, you say you are Abba, even Papa. You've taught me to rest in you. You've taken down the walls around my heart. Now, this hard loss. Satan wants me to believe you're messing me over. I refuse to believe that. You are a good Father. You do not screw around with your kids." I wiped my eyes as I stopped at an intersection.

Pulling into Homer Lake Forest Preserve, I pulled up under a maple tree beside the water and opened the windows. Massaging my neck, I leaned against the seat. The water lapping the dock sounded like God's own heartbeat. "You're right here, aren't you?"

Yes. I could almost see his smile.

"It was such a good place—so close, part-time, and a sliding scale fee. I thought it was your provision." My pulse raced as I blew my nose.

Trust me.

"Yes." In my mind's eye, I climbed into his lap. He put his arm around me as I wept against his shoulder. The fresh air blowing off the lake mingled with my sense of his scent. Above me, in the maple, a cardinal twittered.

As I drove back into town that day, I considered my options. I could keep my five clients from the agency. My office could be my living room. Marketing my own private practice would take time, but I could work part-time and offer a sliding scale.

The next day I ate lunch with Bonnie. "I could see clients in my bedroom, I guess. Oh, I mean my living room. But that says it all, doesn't it?" I grinned. "Maybe that's not such a good idea." My Freudian slip showed my unease with seeing clients at my own home.

"Maybe not," she agreed. "Any other group practices you could join?"

"Mulrooney and Associates has just opened an office in St. Joe. After the second psychosis, I saw Larry from that group a couple of times. Maybe they have an opening."

"It's a plan." We disposed of our lunch debris and emerged into the fall sunlight. Under the colorful maple leaves, Bonnie hugged me. "Something will work out."

"Well, God has to do it. I don't see anywhere I can work part-time and offer clients a sliding scale fee." I opened my palms to the sky and shrugged.

A few days later, I contacted Dr. Mulrooney. I liked the idea of "once a client of the agency; now on staff." After my first meeting, when he said, "You pray about joining us and we will, too," it seemed completely right. He was a strong, prayerful leader.

But after several meetings, I realized I couldn't work with him. He would dominate me. I wasn't strong enough. I would feel as powerless as I did with my father. Though I was attracted to that emotional dynamic at first, I soon understood it wouldn't be good for me. In graduate school, I'd learned about Freud's repetition compulsion. Dr. Freud said we tend to recreate the atmosphere of our childhood, even if it is unhealthy, hoping for a different outcome. The repetition compulsion is the basis of the saying: "The definition of insanity is doing the same thing over and over and expecting a different result." Just in time, God whispered to me, *Don't do it*. I sensed God's fathering. He'd steered me away from a situation in which I wouldn't thrive.

I headed toward Homer Lake on another prayer drive. It was December. I pulled across route 130 onto the country road. The sun glittered on the crust of ice on the roadway. I tensed as the car slipped. "Papa, I know joining that group would have been as tense as driving on ice. But what else is there? Where else can I go? I thought this was from you."

I struggled along, seeing the five clients I had, in my living room. None of them was seriously disturbed, so I felt safe enough. When my first client, an artist, moved, he created a painting of the Holy Spirit shining on us as we talked, with a confused tangle of lines in the upper left. The upper right showed a straight road, with pines lining the way. The artistic representation of the progress he'd made in therapy encouraged me. God had used me to help straighten out his life.

And I continued to pray about my career. With tears, I wrote on November 4, 1987:

Papa, you know my struggles, my confusion, and my pain. I need the ability to mourn the losses I feel now. I need encouragement about my gifting. I want to give you my fear that I won't succeed in this profession, that I'll go back to being a secretary or a seamstress or a sales clerk, and I don't feel called to any of those.

I want to use what you have worked into my life to help others grow. I want to teach them what you've taught me. Writing, leading retreats, speaking, all seem to require a more entrepreneurial spirit than establishing a private practice, and I have so little of the self-confidence and drive of an entrepreneur. You must do it! Whatever it is, you must do it!

Then, the next day, I boldly wrote another prayer, asking for specific job parameters:

Jesus, because I've seen you respond to specific requests before, I want to ask some specific things in this wilderness. If you want me to continue in a generalist counseling direction, I would like you to provide an office to do it from. Ideally, I'd like my own space with secretarial service . . . . I do ask for a sublease for two days and an evening, with access to a typewriter and a copier. You know me, Papa, and you care about me, and you are working good things in my life and my heart. I need your grace to see your hand and your heart.

As I worked on relaxing and trusting God with my job, I noticed other areas of more peace, especially with Jerry. We had joined a small group at NCF, but after a few years, he refused to be in a group with me. He said he felt judged and controlled by me. I'd slowly begun to see how my corrections and additions to his communications hurt him. I needed to let him be himself.

In early November 1987, we were asked to make an announcement at church about an upcoming workday with Empty Tomb. In our early years together, Jerry had pounded many nails at their Saturday workdays. We generated a few questions for me to ask him in front of the congregation. That's how we'd make the announcement at the end of service.

The night before, we read the newspaper in the living room. "Can we rehearse these questions?"

Jerry glanced at me over the top of the sports page. "I don't think we need to. You ask them, I'll answer them."

"Really? Don't you want to rehearse your answers?"

"No, I'm good." He smiled. "I know you don't like that, but it'll be okay."

"Okay." I grinned at him. It's his show, I thought, as I picked up the "Living" section of the newspaper.

The next day, in front of the congregation, he answered my questions with no editorial comments from me. He took my hand as we walked out of church. "You did great. You didn't correct me once! Thanks!"

"You didn't need any help from me. You were fine. I'm getting it, aren't I?"

"Yup, you really are. You're starting to be fun to live with." He grinned. I knew he was thinking of our early morning lovemaking before church. He was also referencing the title of a book I'd read ten years ago, *Are You Fun to Live With?*[5] I hadn't been fun for a long time as I struggled through these last ten years. But I was getting there. Even our sex life was better.

I was accepting myself and my life as God ordained it. I grieved the "perfection" of the job situation with Elaine. I worked on believing that God had something better. Remembering the Assembly of God's foreign missions secretary Charles Greenaway's phrase, "Our God can, our God will, and if not he has something better," I thought about how God had worked out the Psychological Clinic job that had been such a good transition from housewife to therapist. Surely, he has not brought me this far to drop me. I'd learned that from Irene at UAG during those rides in the country where she'd listened to me and shared her wisdom.

On November 16, 1987, I wrote in my journal: "Father, I give you permission to do anything you want with me. I assume whatever you do or allow will be for your glory and my ultimate joy. Love, Karen."

Father-God was bringing me into a deeper faith. My struggle now was that he was too good to be true. Does he really mean to carry me through this anxiety to the promised land of peace and joy? Anxiety had been such a part of my life, I felt nervous without it. But the Bible promised peace, and I was determined to enjoy peace. Peace required believing God was a true Papa-God. And that his plans for my life were worth what they cost both him and me.

An experience with Jennifer that winter gave me additional perspective on God's heart. I had decided she needed to walk to junior high school, a distance of less than a mile. One cold morning she resisted. "It's too cold. Drive me!" she said, as she sat on her bed, hunched over in her heavy jacket.

"No, you can do it. It's good for you to know you can endure the cold." I walked back into the kitchen and started running hot water to wash dishes. Pretty soon I heard the front door slam. "God, it's so hard to make Jennifer do hard things." Tears burned my eyes. "She gets so angry." I pondered it all day. In the evening, I wrote:

God is in exactly the same predicament. There is no way he can genuinely communicate the higher purposes that allowing free will and hence suffering, serves in the system. He can only say: "Eye hath not seen, nor ear heard, neither has it entered into the heart of man, all that God has prepared for those who love him."

How I longed this morning to be able to make Jenny understand the higher purposes in her suffering, but she does not have the capacity to understand. I'm tempted to question why God makes us like this, but that is itself a part of the suffering, it seems. I am not in charge, and the only sane choice is wholehearted submission to who he is. He has proven his love to me on the cross and is therefore trustworthy.

More and more, I leaned on his heart. Since March when I'd acknowledged still hating my father, I'd prayed daily to be delivered. One morning in November, I woke up and sensed peace where the hatred had been. I jumped out of bed. The sun warmed my face as I stood at the south window. "God, I don't know how you've done it, but you have taken that hatred." An image of my heart floated into my mind. The big weed was gone. Unlike the barren winter landscape outside my window, lilies and roses were pushing up through the soil of my heart. "Glory! Papa, you have done it," I whispered. "You are Deliverer. Hallelujah!"

That November, inspired by Joan Beck's alphabet-organized Thanksgiving column in the *Chicago Tribune*, I wrote the first of ten yearly prayers:

> Father God, our help in ages past, our hope in years to come, thank you for apples and air, for bears and bodies and cucumbers, and cantaloupe. For French fries and David; for daffodils and Faust. For grace and greatness and glory.
>
> You who are our mighty fortress, I thank you for hippopotamuses and highlands and hallelujahs! For inspiration and incarnation! For joy and jubilance! For Jerry and Jenny and Karen—and Libby. For mountains and marriage. For onomatopoeia and onions.
>
> You who are the Rock of Ages, cleft for us, I thank you for potpourri and pineapple and Pollyanna and potatoes. For possibilities. For psychological tests and quinine and queens and quince. For rabbits and revelation and remembering. For summer and seasoning; for squash and supper. And sanity!
>
> There is no God like you—there is no other Rock! For which I thank you! And, I thank you for theology and tumescence and targets and tulips. For underpasses and Valium, for water and exits and zoos!

And, I thank you for Jesus, risen. And for righteousness that is a gift because of our choice to believe, not a wage that we earn. And for angels, and for waiting, with hope.

The last page of my second journal, from early 1988, ends with Psalm 56:12–13:

I am under vows to you, oh God; I will present my thank offerings to you.

For you have delivered me from death and my feet from stumbling, that I may walk before God in the light of life.

You have done it, Papa—you have truly "touched my intensity with joy!"

You've delivered me from the hatred.
You've filled me with thanksgiving.
You, alone, are worthy.

PART III

ABUNDANCE
BEYOND BELIEF

CHAPTER 18

PAPA'S TENDER HEART

By the fall of 1987, after ten years of working through the deep wounds and lies of the sexual abuse, I'd begun to trust God's tenderness. When the Communication Center broke up, I grieved the loss and trusted. When working for Dr. Mulrooney didn't work out, I felt God's fathering. Though I still felt anxious about my career, I clung to the image of Jesus holding my father and me, weeping. I can trust a God who suffers with me. And when I saw the film *The Mission* that October, he showed me even more powerfully his fellowship in our suffering.

In the film, based on a true story, a small Catholic mission is established in the jungle. The mission brings not only Christianity but also art and music to the residents. But in the end, the mission is destroyed. The Catholic authorities knew of and could have stopped the destruction, but chose not to. A last scene shows a broken violin piece in the river, floating away.

Films rarely affect me. This one, though, exposed a wound. One day, a few years after my father's first abuse in the cornfield, he told me he'd confessed to Father Wright, our parish priest, what he'd done. I was a kid. I didn't understand the implications of his confession.

When I saw that broken violin piece swept away with the current, however, the injustice of the mission's destruction merged with my own residual sense of injustice. Like the bishops in the movie, Father Wright knew. And he could have intervened. The pastoral leader of our parish knew of a father's violation and, as far as I know, did nothing.

I stomped around my kitchen that October night of 1987. "God, where are you in injustice? I want a dream!" I'd never asked so boldly.

In a dream that night, I was a prisoner of war. First, a uniformed officer taunted me with questions about my supposedly illegal activities, but I felt completely composed. Brandishing a braided leather whip, he stepped toward me. As he raised the whip, another man, already bloody, stepped up to take my blows with me.

I woke up before the first strike. I lay still, staring into the darkness. Slowly, I turned my head. It was 3:00 A.M. Wow. He really gave me a dream. That man who stepped up is Jesus. He takes the unjust blows with us.

Dear God, Papa, you are worth what you cost. You will provide all I need. A place to practice psychotherapy. Calmness of heart. Ability to parent Jenny and be a good wife to Jerry. Oh, the deep, deep love of Jesus!

The next day, my mother called. They were going to celebrate their fiftieth wedding anniversary early, in late October, before they went to New Mexico for the winter. We chatted for a few moments, and she gave me the details for the event. As I clicked off the phone, I thought, I feel good. I don't have that weight in my chest I always have after talking to my mother. I no longer want something from her. She doesn't have the nurture I need. I have Libby and I have Jerry. Well, the anniversary party will be the acid test. We'll see how I feel then.

When the day of the party came, we pulled up to the small white church. I waved to a cousin as we emerged from our blue Honda. Jerry and Jenny walked ahead, holding hands, as I hung back to peruse the stained glass windows. My friend Mercedes, a good photographer, had taken our wedding portrait below the third window. Though

I'd never sung "Jesus loves me, this I know," in this wood-framed church, my spirit had been imbued with the majesty of God. As I studied the once familiar building, I thought, Protestants tend to think they can figure God out. Catholics know more of his mystery. It felt good to remember something positive from my Catholic upbringing.

"Hey, are you coming in or not?" My sister Nancy and brother-in-law, Joe, had walked up behind me.

"Oh, yeah, just thinking. How are you guys?" They fell into step with me.

"Good. Haven't seen you in a while." Joe opened the door for us into the Father Wright parish hall. At the sight of his name, I saw the image from *The Mission*, of the broken violin piece floating in the water. Just as quickly, I thought, God has made up to me the years the locusts have eaten. As I hung my jacket in the entryway, I smiled. God does all things well. The women of the church were setting out roast beef, mashed potatoes and gravy, pies and cakes. The smells of the familiar food of my childhood drew me in.

I hadn't been in this room since my own wedding fifteen years before. I walked into the bathroom and saw the familiar steel-enclosed stalls, the porcelain sink under a metal-encased mirror, and the small window facing the parking lot, which let in some of the bright fall sunshine. Here I had dressed in the gown I'd made of chiffon and my grandmother's crocheted lace. It seemed a lifetime ago.

I emerged from the bathroom and looked around. There must be seventy people here. My classmate Suzie's mother was sitting at one of the long tables covered with long sheets of white paper arranged in the length of the terrazzo-floored room. I'd heard Suzie had died a few years ago of breast cancer. I walked up to her. "I'm so sorry to hear of Suzie's death."

"Thanks." She smiled briefly.

I'd never spoken to her before. Suzie had been one of the golden girls of my childhood, a sidekick to Ruth Ann, who'd laughed at my giggle on the playground. We exchanged a few more pleasantries before I stepped into a corner.

A flock of memories flew through my mind. I'd never been to Suzie's house. But she'd been part of the Catholic Youth Organization (CYO). We'd square-danced on this terrazzo floor. I'd felt part of the group, dancing, swirling to and fro on the smooth surface. One winter, the CYO had skated on the ice at the local swimming lake. The group had included Catholic youth from other school districts. Although I'd felt rejected by the Halesburg teenagers, a couple of the out-of-district boys had skated with me that night.

Closing my eyes, I could almost smell the hot chocolate we shared around a fire on the banks of the lake. CYO was where I'd met Jane, who along with her friend Mary had been my roommates the first year of college.

In addition to CYO, 4-H had planted seeds of hope. I remembered holding hands with sweet George as we walked the downtown Chicago streets on that high school trip. For the first time that day, I had felt pretty. *Papa, you did provide a measure of hope in the desert of my childhood. Thank you.*

"Hey, are you gonna join the party?" My brother interrupted my musing. I took the glass of punch he offered.

"Hey, how are you?" We'd visited Craig a few years ago in Connecticut. Still a pilot, he'd taken us up in his helicopter for an aerial view of the city.

The last summer I lived at home, when I returned from the Drama Institute in upstate New York, after my freshman year, he had made living at home bearable. Neither of us talked seriously, but the evening rides in his MGB sports car had given me a feeling of freedom.

Jerry, with Jenny near the front of the buffet line, looked my direction and smiled. Craig and I walked toward them, passing my parents who were seated at a nearby table talking to well-wishers. They didn't look up.

"I sure enjoyed the helicopter ride last year, especially when you let me handle the controls. That was such a strange sensation—it felt so loose, disconnected from the rotor," I said to Craig. We surveyed the slices of apple and lemon meringue pie.

"Yeah, it takes some getting used to." He picked up a slice of apple pie.

The four of us filled our plates and carried them to a table. Craig drifted off to speak to Herb, my oldest brother, while Jerry, Jenny, and I took a seat at an empty table. Another brother, Harold, sat down across from us.

"So, you got your doctorate, did you?" Harold asked. He was the only other sibling who'd garnered any college credits. His education, though, had been cut short by his schizophrenic diagnosis. He had been in and out of institutions for the past twenty-five years.

I laughed. "Not doctorate, just Master of Social Work."

"Oh, I see. Very good. It's all just common sense, isn't it?"

"Common sense? I think an M.S.W. is a little more than that." Harold sounds like my father, I thought. That's not just my mentally ill brother's idea. My father has such a need to feel okay about himself, he denigrates other's accomplishments. Sad.

Sad, too, to see Harold, still stuck in an endless cycle of breakdowns. What was the difference between him and me? I'd been just as disturbed as he was. Jerry and I had visited one Saturday at the farm the first year we'd been married. Harold had been living at home for a few months, but at the time we visited, he was developing psychotic symptoms again. He'd returned from a motorcycle ride with a yellow wastebasket he'd picked up by the side of the road. It matched the yellow of the motorcycle's gas tank. Jerry and I were sorting apples to make cider, out near the driveway. Harold had pulled to a stop beside us. "Look, both yellow."

"O-kay," I said, glancing at Jerry to gauge his reaction. Jerry hadn't been around Harold much and wasn't familiar with his symptoms.

"So what?" Jerry said, frowning.

"The sun is going to keep shining," Harold said as he turned toward the house.

As I remembered the yellow wastebasket incident, I thought, I'd made similar odd connections when I was psychotic. But I'd recovered and even gone on to learn the psychiatric name for deriving extraordinary meaning from ordinary objects: ideas of reference.

What I learned in graduate school was not just "common sense." I'd learned a specialized vocabulary and a body of clinical understanding.

Combined with my own hard-won emotional wisdom, that knowledge guided my therapeutic thinking. My father and my brother didn't even try to understand me. Oh, well, that's just the way it is. They don't get it.

As I easily chatted with old neighbors and acquaintances about their current activities, I thought: I have truly left home. Previously, returning to Halesburg had meant a regression to old self-consciousness and old roles. But I'd left behind the old self-rejection, the hatred, and much of the anxiety. That day, I was a different person—full of peace. I felt as fluid as I looked in my silky dress.

And though I had received a God of judgment in this place, I had returned knowing a God of grace. Mysterious and just, yes—but not sadistic—not waiting for me to screw up so he could punish me. The real God is not the abuser my father was, nor the guilt-inducer Father Wright had been. The real God is Papa-God. His lap is safe, his grace is encompassing, and his ear is attuned to my deepest needs.

I approached my father, holding court at the end of one of the long tables, across from my mother. I stopped between them.

"What a nice crowd. You must be happy to see everyone," I said, glancing around.

"Oh, hi, Karen. How are you? How's your family?" Mom spoke. My father glanced up from his roast beef.

"We're good. How are you guys feeling?" Health was always a safe topic. I looked at them. They both showed the effects of the sun from their New Mexico winters. My mother's soft hair contrasted with her leathery face. My father's usually straggly hair had been cut and, for once, he was clean.

I thought, I do not belong to them. I belong to Jesus. God's protection and provision have sufficed. *Thank you, Jesus.*

"We're pretty good, for our age." My father spoke up. He looked me up and down. "You look like you've lost weight."

"No, just a new dress." I smiled as I ran my hand down my skirt. Previously, his comments on my body left me feeling invaded. That day I shrugged it off. I couldn't stop him looking. I could stop his impact.

After the prophetic dream and my peacefulness at the anniversary party, God strengthened me to trust him for my work. I couldn't find a place to work part-time and offer a sliding-scale fee, so I continued to see a few clients at home for the next several months. Especially after I hired a seasoned therapist to supervise my work, my anxiety level became more manageable. Her supervision helped me see both my competence and my growing edges.

In July, 1989, a therapist I knew from UAG invited me to join the Christian Counseling Center. They were located in a church across town, but I could offer clients manageable fees and work part-time. The agency had a secretary and I could have my own space, just like I'd asked God for. Again he'd shown himself a Father who provides.

In the strength that God had worked into my heart, I finally confronted my father with the consequences of his abuse, thirty-six years after the fact. In 1991, six years before the garden confrontation when I learned of the rape, I sent this letter:

Dear Dad,

I've always felt like one of the unspoken rules in our family is "don't talk about what you really think or feel." I'm writing this letter to break that rule for myself, and to do so creates a fair amount of anxiety for me. But it is finally important enough to speak honestly and to risk whatever your response or nonresponse may be.

I want to tell you something about what life was like for me, growing up in the family, both the things that I appreciate and the things that brought great pain. I appreciate that you worked so hard on the farm and the other jobs to provide for us. I'm glad I grew up on a farm rather than in the inner city, where poverty has a much harsher face. I'm glad for the stability of living in the same house, the same community all those years, and even now, knowing that the farm is there means something good to me.

I appreciate your financial generosity, even when you couldn't give much—like when I was in college. I'm glad you went to church regularly and acknowledged God's existence. I imagine you have prayed for me a great deal over the years, and I'm grateful for those prayers. I'm glad you and Mom have stayed together. All these things are good and helpful to me.

And yet, there are other aspects of our relationship that have created great pain in my life and I have often wondered how much you understand about your effect on me. I remember several instances of sexual abuse, but the one in the cornfield when I was four and the one when we went turtle-hunting when I was twelve have been particularly devastating memories. I felt used and objectified—like I was not even a person. You must have been abused in some way yourself to do those things to me. I wish you would have faced your own pain rather than acting it out on me.

There's a lot more I'd like to say to you, but I'd like to hear what your response is to this letter first. If you choose not to respond, I will know that that really is your choice, and I won't always wonder what could have happened if I'd tried to be honest with you.

I wish you wanted to know me, Dad. I wish you'd ask my forgiveness for the sexual abuse. I wish you would, even now, face your own pain.

I wish you God's best.

Karen

I was rarely depressed in those days. Waiting for his response, though, I fell into a depressive pattern of sleeping and eating too much. Confronting him had required an enormous amount of emotional energy. I was depleted.

After two weeks, he wrote a two word response: "I'm sorry." But he wasn't sorry enough to engage in real discussion. He wasn't sorry enough to explore his own motivation. He wasn't sorry enough to hear my pain. My depression lifted. I had done my part to try to reconcile. I'd exposed my heart to him. In response, he gave me two words. Admittedly, they were the necessary words. But they were not sufficient. Two words were not enough to build on. I'd often fantasized a warm relationship with him. Now I could deal with the reality. My father would not pay the price.

Some of us will never confront those who've hurt us. Perhaps they're dead, they're not safe enough, or we're unconvinced of the value of confrontation. If we choose to call them to account, we need to be prepared for the consequences. Very few perpetrators take responsibility. Many deny they did anything wrong. Others, like my father, recognize the wrong, but won't engage.

By the time I risked confrontation, I had already traded fathers. Father-God had pulled the weeds that had grown from my earthly father's abuse. Then he'd seeded the holes in my heart with his flowers. By the time I attempted to reconcile with my father, I was living among the lilies.

Our Forever Father allows difficult tests in our lives that expose the weeds in our hearts. However, unlike many of our natural fathers, Papa-God suffers through the trials with us, revealing his compassionate heart. And sometimes, testing just exposes the lilies.

CHAPTER 19

PAPA TESTS
MY HEALED HEART

W hat brings you to therapy?" I had just begun my first session with "Alice," at 1:30, July 9, 1992, when I heard a knock at my office door. "I'm sorry, usually we don't get interrupted."

Nanette, the Counseling Center secretary, stood at the door, her face pale and tight. "Public works is on the phone," she said. "There's been an accident."

"Oh!" I pushed past her, running to the phone in her office, the sudden adrenalin nearly cutting off my breath. Has it happened, is he dead? Jerry was now an electrician for Urbana public works. I thought he took too many chances. When he'd worked with the private company before taking the city job, he often hooked up electrical services without cutting power. Too many times, I'd imagined getting news of his death.

"What's happened?"

"Jerry's had an accident. You need to get to Carle Hospital as soon as possible."

"Where should I go?"

"He's in the ER, ma'am."

Oh, of course, stupid question. I ran to get my purse, leaving Nanette to explain to my client. Of all days to have the old VW van! It's so slow. I could get there in ten minutes in the Honda, but Jenn has that at work. I jumped into the VW and pulled onto Windsor Road. "Jesus, Jesus, is he alive? The guy didn't say. Oh, God. Sweet Jesus, our lives are in your hands!" I pounded my fist on the steering wheel as my tears gushed. "If twenty years is all I get with him, so be it." Gripping the wheel, I thought, I really am living among God's lilies. "Thank you, Jesus, that submission is my first thought at a time like this."

As I chugged across town, my thoughts turned to our twentieth anniversary weekend in Saugatuck, Michigan, a month earlier. Remembering the rainy walk down the street of elegant houses overlooking Lake Michigan, my tears flowed. The bike ride on Saturday. That house at the turn of the Kalamazoo River—its New England architecture that reminded us of other wonderful vacations. We didn't have a cross word with each other the whole weekend. "Oh, God, please, not now, it's just getting good!"

At the emergency room parking lot, I jumped out, not locking the door. A policeman, who seemed to be waiting for me, took my arm and led me to a private waiting room furnished with two couches, lit by a table lamp. Jerry's supervisor, Allen, sat with his head in his hands. Jenn stood to the side, her long hair disheveled. A chaplain sat across from Allen.

"Is he okay? What happened?" I collapsed next to Allen on the hard couch. I grabbed Jenn as she sat beside me. Though I'd stopped biting my fingernails years before, I chewed a nail.

The chaplain answered: "He's in a coma, but he's alive. They're doing tests now, you can't see him yet." He stood, opening the door. "I'll go check."

"Allen, what happened?"

"We were working on a streetlight circuit that we thought we'd turned off, but somehow, it was still live. I should have known." He put his hands over his red face. His whole body trembled. He turned away.

"It wasn't your fault," I said, touching the back of his shoulder.

I turned to Jenn. "He's gonna be okay, Mom."

I looked at her. Her eyes were red; but her voice was steady. At forty years old, I knew that bad things happened to good people every day, and this might just be our day. But I didn't want to discourage her faith. My faith said Jesus would be with us through anything. I was less sure of getting what we wanted.

"I hope so." Folding a tissue, I wiped my cheeks.

The chaplain returned. "He's holding his own. They're going to transfer him to Springfield to the regional burn unit. You'll be able to see him soon, when they put him in the ambulance."

In the past few years I had gotten close to Sheila. She and her husband Paul led our house church. I phoned her. "Sheila, Jerry's been hurt. He cut into a live streetlight wire. They're taking him to Springfield."

"Is he okay?" I could hear the fright in her voice.

"He's alive. I don't know anything else. Call people to pray, will you?"

"Yes, of course. And I'll drive you."

The chaplain opened the door. "You can see him now. He's still in a coma, with assisted breathing," he warned, as he held the door open.

I walked into the hallway. Jerry lay on a gurney, still as wax, the only movement the technician's hand-operated airflow through the tube down his throat.

I kissed him on the cheek. "I'll see you later. I love you." He did not respond. So this is what he'll look like in his coffin, I thought. But he's alive now. Don't give up hope. I could feel my heart beating. Slow down, trust Papa-God.

In the car with Sheila and Jenn headed toward Springfield, the unknown silenced us. Jerry's stillness on the gurney haunted me. What if he's a vegetable? I could not stop imagining him unresponsive, lying in bed in a nursing home. *No, Jesus, not that. That would be worse than death.*

"Paul is calling people to pray," Sheila said, breaking the silence.

"Thanks." I stared at the gray pavement stretched out ahead of us. "I'm just holding my breath. I guess if he dies before we get there, I couldn't have said goodbye, anyway—he wouldn't be awake. But I'd rather God would take him than leave him a vegetable. He's taken too much electricity. Allen said he had to call on the radio for help, then get into the bucket truck and pull the Illinois Power line fuse before the electricity stopped. That had to take two minutes. The streetlight circuits are wired in series. The amperage is constant, and the voltage varies. It's the amperage that kills. How can he survive?"

Keeping her eyes on the road, Sheila reached over and patted my hand. Across the seat back, Jenn laid her hand on my shoulder. I leaned my head against the headrest. My heart thumped in my chest, and my stomach hurt. I stared at the rows of corn and beans, the landscape of my childhood. I loved the black dirt, the fertility of the soil, the big sky. Though my years at home on the farm had been painful, the pleasures of the creation had sustained me. Fields surrounded the junior college, too, where we had spent our first year together. Homer Lake, where I often went to pray, lay amid grain fields. But no prayers came as we sped toward the fearful future.

After a two-hour journey that felt like half my life, we rushed into Memorial Medical Center. Finding the burn unit, we opened the door only to find a second door with instructions to wash our hands before we entered. We did so quickly and entered the unit. To our left, three nurses stood behind a desk. One of them looked up from her chart as we approached.

"Jerry Rabbitt: Is he alive?" I grasped the counter.

"Yes, he's just been brought up. He's coming out of the coma. You can see him after we get him settled. Come back in an hour, at 6:00." The nurse touched my hand.

"He's still alive. He's still alive." Suddenly weak-kneed, I held onto the counter.

"Let's go down to the cafeteria. Get something to eat." Sheila simultaneously reached for me and put her arm around Jenn. I allowed myself to be pulled away, and we found the elevator.

As the elevator doors closed, I squeezed Jenn's hand. "How are you doing?"

She was breathing shallowly and her face looked a little less smooth than before she walked into the hospital. "I'm okay."

I sat down at a cafeteria table, oblivious to the dinner hour noise of the staff and patients' families, who filled the big open room of hard tables. Sheila and Jenn went to get hamburgers.

He's alive and waking up. *Thank you, Jesus.* I wiped my face with a napkin. But what's next?

We ate, and then returned to the waiting room outside the unit. Sheila and Jenn sat next to each other under the florescent glare. I sat across from them and picked up a *Family Circle* magazine. I stared at a chocolate cake recipe. Would Jerry ever enjoy his favorite chocolate cherry cake again? The nurse said he was waking up. But was he brain-damaged? At that moment, I realized the hamburger was giving me indigestion.

"I need to find a bathroom."

"I saw one in the hall," Sheila said, pointing left.

As I opened the bathroom door after using the facilities, the nurse opened the hall door from the burn unit.

"Oh, there you are. Jerry has some third-degree burns. The electricity entered his hand and exited his thighs. The burns will heal, but it will be up to forty-eight hours before we know about internal damage—to his heart, lungs, kidneys, and other organs."

"Oh." I leaned against the wall. Two days seemed forever to wait before I'd know the shape of the rest of our lives.

"So far, he's doing awfully well. The report we got said he took 6.6 amps for probably two minutes. Five milliamps can kill. It's a miracle he's alive." She touched my shoulder, her face soft.

I stared at her, shaking my head. I couldn't think what to say. I hadn't remembered that the lethal dose of amperage was so small.

"He'll be in the unit about three weeks, recovering. Just take it a day at a time, okay? You and your daughter can have five minutes with him now." We gathered Jenn from the waiting room. I clutched Jenn's hand as the nurse led us past the nurse's station to a glass-walled room. Jerry lay in a hospital bed with the sides up, his right hand hidden under a thick bandage. The hospital smell was stronger inside his room. A breathing tube curved down his throat. The ventilator whooshed. The light was dim. He turned his head as we approached.

"Hi, Jer," I said. I touched his bare shoulder, pulling up the hospital gown.

Jenn stood next to me on the right side of his bed. "Hi Dad," she said. He tried to smile around the tube. His color seemed all right, and he looked alert. His legs lay still under the thin hospital blanket. Except for his right hand, he looked normal. Could he actually be okay? My heart slowed.

He clutched the breathing tube with his left hand.

"You don't want to do that. If you pull it out, they'll have to put it back in while you're awake." I pushed his left hand away from the tube. He didn't resist. He raised his eyebrows.

I handed him a pen and paper.

He wrote on the pad with his unpracticed left hand. "What happened?"

"You cut into a live streetlight wire."

His eyes widened. I squeezed his shoulder.

"You've got burns on your thighs and your hand, and nobody knows about internal damage yet. The nurses say we won't know for twenty-four to forty-eight hours."

He lifted the pen again. "Wheelchair."

I laughed, the tension I'd held for the past six hours draining out. His sense of humor was intact. There couldn't be too much brain damage. He'd often teased me that his time would come; that I'd push him in a wheelchair, like he'd taken care of me during those breakdowns.

Jenn squeezed my hand. I glanced at her. She understood the significance of his little joke, too. A tear rolled down her face now, a counterpoint to her smile. I had hardly stopped crying. Jenn had been dry-eyed. Did seeing her strong father in a hospital bed for the first time shake her faith? Seeing him alive and responsive fed my faith. I took a deep breath.

The nurse interrupted my thoughts. "You'll have to go now. Jerry, here, is in intensive care. Two family members can see him ten minutes every two hours."

"You heard her, Sweetie. I'll be back in two hours, okay? We'll be right outside." I kissed his forehead, running my fingers through his hair. He was alive. He was making jokes. I looked into his soft gray eyes, seeing a future and a hope.

Later, I learned of all those who prayed to the Father-God who gave me that hope. Many prayed when they heard and called others to pray. Even in those days before e-mail, the request was passed around the country in a few hours. That night, Paul and forty others squeezed into a living room to plead for Jerry's life.

He came home in eight days rather than three weeks, though it was three months before he went back to work. During the ordeal, one of the nurses said, "Trauma leaves its mark." The deepest effect of this trauma has been a sweetness in Jerry that I'd never seen before. And God also used it to show my new identity to Jerry. I was no longer a mental patient, wandering in barrenness. I knew God had grown lilies in my heart's desert, but in this crisis, Jerry, too, could see them. I saw a new softness in him while he saw new stability in me.

A few months after Jerry went back to work, God gave me a letter. Driving across town the day of Jerry's accident, I'd submitted to God, not knowing the outcome. I had given up my fight with God about pain. One late winter morning, after Jerry left for work and Jenn for school, I brewed a cup of Constant Comment tea, carried it to the navy couch, and pondered again how God feels about our suffering.

"God, you so shielded Jerry from danger that day. And I sensed your presence so strongly in Springfield. That first night, as I was going to bed, I almost felt your hands as I sensed you cupping my cheeks and kissing my forehead. You are right here. And you suffer with us."

I picked up a legal pad and began writing. Within half an hour I had written, in the form of a letter to a semi-autobiographical twenty-nine-year-old Annie, a treatise on how God views our pain:

The Father of Jesus
1 Golden Way
New Jerusalem

My dearest Annie:

I know you are unsure of me these days, particularly wondering whether you really are dear to me. Your twenties have been such painful years, haven't they? I know you've wondered whether you would ever stop crying. And those breakdowns that landed you in the hospital—such terror—thinking you were going to be rolled up in a little ball and thrown out into the empty universe. I'm so sorry you had to go through all that. My heart has bled for you.

You've been wrestling with me these days. You don't know how important that struggling is to me. I will always rather fight with you than to watch you walk away. Please keep telling me how you feel. You seem to understand that you have to keep wrestling if you ever want to make sense of these difficult years.

You've particularly been wrestling with me about free will. I wanted to write to you today because you've begun to see it differently. Up until now you've always said, "Free will isn't worth what it costs! It was a human choice in the garden that led to all this pain, and it was my father's choices that have provoked so much terror in my life."

You've blamed me for creating such a system. You admitted to me two weeks ago Saturday that you actually hated me. (I was so glad to hear you confess that!) And now, in these last two weeks, it has begun to dawn on you that there's no real goodness on earth without real evil. The same ability to choose that creates evil also yields goodness. Do you get it, really? I want people who will love me freely, without coercion or manipulation. That means you all need to have a choice to walk with me or to walk away from me. I know it's confusing, too, because it's hard for you to evaluate who's with me and who's not. Like your father, who looked like he was walking with me but sure walked away from me that day in the cornfield when he molested you.

Have you ever thought about what I felt that day? I know you've been angry with me about how I've set up the system, but think about it from my point of view: I want a family to love. So I made Adam and Eve with the ability to be my children. But they walked away from me and unleashed such evil and suffering. How I grieved! I was sorry I'd made them. Every violent thought broke my heart. And that's how I felt that day in the cornfield. I wept over you both, knowing what your father's sin would cost in your life, and in his. And, do you see that I could not intervene? If I stopped your father, it would only be fair to stop all the evil choices and then where would human choice be and then how would I get my family? I want a family! I want an enormous, extended family. I want people who want to come to family reunions.

Well, it's not that I couldn't intervene in the most literal sense—I could, of course. What I mean is, if I did routinely stop bad choices, that would be the end of choice. Real choices require real consequences. Maybe you think I could just make you love me, but I want a family who really loves me.

But let me tell you, it was excruciating for me to restrain myself. It would have been much easier to stop your father. It is the thought of that glorious family reunion that sustains me.

I mean, imagine what it would be like for you to hold your three-year-old daughter while she had a bone marrow tap. You could hardly stand it, could you? You'd be able to stand it only if you believed that procedure was the only way to cure her disease. You could hold your screaming daughter only if you understood the purpose; and, even then, you could barely endure not intervening. Well, I can barely stand not stopping human choice, either, but it is the only way to accomplish my purpose.

So, I wanted to write this letter now because you are beginning to understand the value of free will. I want you to understand the next piece, too, that human choice costs me more than it costs any

of you. You've understood Jesus' cross, somewhat—
that I had to lose a part of myself so that we could
gain a new life together. You've grasped that I had to
suffer for you; I don't think you've quite understood
that I also suffer with you.

And you just have to trust me about whether
the purpose is worth the pain.

But try to understand, I'm neither a masoch-
ist nor a sadist. I don't allow such evil because
I find pleasure in pain, either mine or yours. I
suffer, and I ask you to suffer with me, for a life
together that I know will be worth what it costs
both of us.

Bless you, dear one.

I love you,
Papa

Wow. I reread the letter, adding a word here,
taking out a word there. I wrapped my hands around
the ceramic mug and raised it to my chest. Though
the tea had cooled, I felt warm inside. Tears of joy
streamed down my face. I'd never experienced
anything like that writing before. It was as if the
Holy Spirit had hold of the pen. Succinctly, it
expressed what I'd struggled for fifteen years to
grasp. I stretched out on the couch, clasping my
hands behind my head. *My God, my God, you have
never forsaken me.*

In my mind's eye, I saw Jesus kneel next to the couch and lay his head on my chest. I saw myself hug him to my breast, feeling the strength of his shoulders, the comfort of his beating heart, and the scent of his breath. Again, I thought: I can trust someone who suffers with me. God's first word to describe himself in Exodus 34:6 is *compassionate*. That means, "to suffer with." Isaiah 63:9 says, "In all their distress he too was distressed." When Lazarus died, Jesus wept with the mourners. And Jesus says in Matthew 25:40, "Whatever you did for one of the least of these brothers of mine, you did for me." He is so close to those who suffer that he says we relieve his pain when we relieve their pain. How can God truly love us and not suffer with us? *Sweet Jesus. Dear Papa. Holy Spirit.*

God sees the whole picture. He knows his purposes. If he, too, is willing to pay the price, his purpose must be worth the cost. Even sexual abuse. Even mental illness. And the deep loneliness of growing up without feeling understood. Leslie Weatherhead was a British pastor during World War II. In a slim book called, *When the Lamp Flickers,* he says the clearest sentence I've ever read about the relationship of God's power to God's purpose: "Action that defeats purpose is weakness."[6]

We may think God's power or his love is insufficient because he doesn't rescue us from others' sins against us. But if God always rescued us, it would defeat his larger purpose of creating a family who freely chooses to return his love. Rather, his power is in his ability to restrain himself from rescue in order to fulfill his purpose. He wants to give those who walk with him—his family—his own joy. He wants to rejoice with us as we share that love and joy with each other. Weatherhead goes on to point out that that restraint is not weakness. He restrained himself from intervening when they put his dear son to merciless death on a cross. But that restraint is God's power for salvation (2 Cor 13:4). How God's creative sovereignty and human free will work together, I don't know, but these thoughts quiet my mind. His compassion quiets my heart.

In the spring of 1993, the Christian Counseling Center relocated to a two-story house on my side of town, three blocks past where the Communication Center had been. I framed Monet prints and one of my own sunflower photographs to hang on the walls of my little office, upstairs from the waiting room. The receptionist welcomed clients in a wood-trimmed room adjoining the solid wood staircase. I felt like I'd come home, to a place God had prepared just for me. And, over the next few years, as I saw clients get free of lies and grab hold of God's truth, my work anxiety subsided. My real, Forever Father had provided.

Jenn succeeded in college at Southern Illinois University, and Jerry and I grew closer and more playful. One summer day, on break from college, Jenn drove into the backyard just as I was running out of the screen door to evade Jerry's water gun attack. She climbed out of the old blue Honda, watching us with wide eyes. "What are you guys doing?"

"Playing." I giggled as I turned to pelt Jerry with my own stream of water. He'd stopped on the landing outside the screen door, shooting a steady stream of water that reached me eight feet away. Jenn jumped out of the way, watching as we soaked each other and laughed until our bellies ached.

"Since when do you guys play with squirt guns?" She stared at us as if she'd never seen us before.

"Since your father nearly died! Everybody should have a near-death experience. It's done wonders for your dad!"

"Yeah, we're thinking of opening a business. 'Near-Death Experience, Inc.—the best worst thing that'll ever happen to you.'"

"We'll have trouble getting liability insurance, though." Laughing, I grabbed Jenn, putting my cheek next to hers. Jerry wrapped his arms around us both, laying his head on top of ours. We clutched each other, dripping and swaying, under the warm sun.

The warmth between Jerry and me continued to deepen in the next few years. By 1997 when Jerry and I learned of the rape that had been my conception, the news only bolstered my sense of God as my true Father. Knowing I was a product of rape just increased the awe I'd first encountered during the healing of memories prayer time with Paul and Bonnie in January of 1987. That egg and that sperm were the only way to get me. God wanted me. Yes, I'd suffered abuse, neglect, and serious mental illness. But that suffering had only pushed me harder into God's heart. In his compassionate heart, I found myself.

CHAPTER 20

MORE THAN I EVER IMAGINED

God, what should I write to my father on his birthday?" In the corner of my bedroom, I leaned back in my office chair to gaze out the window. It was October 2001. His 86th birthday was the 19th. Usually I wrote, on a blank card, variations of "Have a good day." Today, I sensed God wanted me to write something deeper.

After my father's scene in the garden four years earlier, little had changed in our relationship. One slight shift, though, had occurred. During our visit last June, they had asked us to pray for their failing health. They'd never seemed to value our Protestant prayer before. I felt a bit more accepted, more like they believed we were on the same page with them spiritually. Though he was a lifelong Catholic, I'd heard him speak of his fear of death. That conflict seemed like a continuing manifestation of his two-sided nature. On the one hand, he abused power in the most evil ways. On the other hand, he was a man of prayer, always saying grace before meals, never missing Sunday mass.

Finally, I typed: "I hope you have a good birthday. You've always struck me as both very spiritual and very fearful. John 3:17 says Jesus came into the world not to condemn us but to save us. May that be a comfort to you."

As I printed out the card, I thought, well, that's the most compassionate thing I've ever said to him. I wonder how he'll respond.

Seven days later, I sat down to open a letter from him. He wrote that I was "critical, insulting, and arrogant." He said I had no business telling him what to meditate on. And he didn't appreciate a "holy roller" telling him what to do.

I leaned back in my chair, putting the letter on the end table. My goodness! *Jesus, how sad. I did nothing wrong here, and I get slapped in the face. It's just like the abuse.* A single tear wet my cheek as I got up and went to the kitchen table. Munching a chocolate chip cookie, I thought, he can't tolerate the truth about himself. Was I wrong? I didn't think so. A few years ago, he had an aortic aneurysm. From what Mom reported, he had panic attacks then. Even if I was wrong, why not write: "I don't think I'm as fearful as you say. And yes, isn't it wonderful that Jesus doesn't come to condemn but to save?" Why be so cruel?

The healing image of Jesus weeping with my father and me in the cornfield flitted through my mind. Well, I don't want to be cruel back. I found a stationary pad and wrote: "I'm sorry you felt so hurt by my words. I had no intention of hurting you."

On Thanksgiving, Jerry and I were sitting at the kitchen table when the phone rang. I was tearing bread for the stuffing, and Jerry was chopping celery. Wiping my hands, I picked up the phone to hear my mother's unusually perky voice. I stood in the kitchen doorway, listening to her chatter, raising my eyebrows at Jerry. After a short, mostly one-sided, conversation, I clicked off the phone. "That was weird. Mom was all cheerful, chatting about going to New Mexico. Dad was in the background, making jokes."

"No reference to the letters?"

"As if they never happened." I shook my head.

That was our last significant exchange. Within a few months my father died of a stroke, and the next fall my mother died of lung cancer. To the end, my father felt treacherous to me. And yet, I believe his sin, like mine, is absorbed on Jesus' cross. When I think of him now, I imagine a completely different scene:

Like so many times on the farm, I see my father working in a garden. I see myself approaching him. He doesn't see me coming because he's leaning into the massive rose bush that arches over the entrance to the apple orchard. He's picking red roses, adding to the bundle already in his arm. His dark hair is trim; his khaki shorts display strong legs. As I get nearer, I smell a heavenly scent, such a contrast to his earthy old man smell. He senses me behind him and turns, a smile lighting his face.

Dropping the roses, he reaches for me. "Snooks! You're here. I've been waiting for you."

I rush toward him. Against his shoulder, my voice muffled, I say, "I have waited all my life for your arms." My shoulders shake against his chest as he strokes my hair.

"Yes. I'm so sorry. Satan had such influence on me down there. But God's purposes stand."

"Yes. Here we are. It is finished."

"And I'm so proud of you. You have done so well, my daughter. Have you been to see Papa yet?"

"No, I was sent here first." I look around the garden where we stand, hand in hand. It looks strangely familiar. Rows of apple trees beyond us. At our feet, balloon flowers are in bud. Cardinals flit from tree to rose bush.

"Where is Papa-God? And where's Mom? Is she close?"

"Here they come, now."

I look where he's pointing. My mother, her dark hair flowing behind her, runs toward us. Behind her, a luminous figure approaches more slowly.

"Mommy!" She sweeps me into an embrace, and we swirl around a golden delicious tree. Then, hand in hand with my redeemed father and mother, we kneel before the good Father of us all.

Someone might ask, "How is it that I imagine an abuser in heaven?" How do I imagine any sinner in heaven? My father believed Jesus paid the price for his sin. Though he resisted the intimacy of real reconciliation, he sought forgiveness from me and from God. Every Sunday at Mass, he confessed Jesus as Lord, and he believed in the Resurrection. Romans 10:9: "If you confess with your mouth, 'Jesus is Lord,' and believe in your heart that God raised him from the dead, you will be saved."

Though my father was a deeply conflicted man, I believe he was counting, as I am, on the sacrifice of Jesus. By that sacrifice, we will kneel together before the God who has redeemed our sin.

Now, as I live out the final third of my life, my Forever Father holds my hand. Like a flower gardener, he has grown his daffodils, roses, and lilies in my heart. When he first put plow to soil, the ground of my heart was dry, hard, and full of weeds. The breakdowns in my twenties broke up that ground of shame and pride and grew a daffodil of humility. In the softer soil, he began to pull dozens of weeds. Weeds of my unforgiveness and hatred. Weeds of Satan's lies, planted in the childhood traumas. Lies about rejection and abandonment, worthlessness and fear.

At the same time, he sowed his seeds of truth. The truth about his love, the truth about my memories. The truth of peace that only he can give. He's provided all I need. He has protected what he has planted. He has confronted my weeds and comforted my heart with his tender care. Had I not traded fathers, my life would have been overrun with weeds, planted by the Father of Lies, taking his opportunity from my father's sin. Satan does not grow flowers.

But now, I think of myself as four years old again. As I walk, holding my good Father's hand, he and I enjoy the new flowers springing up in my heart. The biggest patch of new flowers contains the roses and lilies of writing and speaking. For many years, images of writing and speaking populated the back of my mind. With my parents in God's good hands, those images pushed to the forefront.

Except for a poem about breaking up with Roger when I was eighteen, published in the junior college literary magazine, my creative writing had been limited to personal journaling. I'd done more speaking, beginning in the early nineties. My first speaking engagements had been with the Communication Center. Then, from 1996 to 1998, a colleague and I offered several seminars through the Christian Counseling Center. I also led a number of women's retreats at NCF. But writing seemed out of reach.

However, four years before my parents' deaths, on a hot Friday in 1998, in western Illinois, I stood in the back of the tent at the Cornerstone Festival during a writing seminar. I'd been coming to this gathering of thousands of Christian campers every year since I'd first taken Jenn seven years before. I loved the vitality and safety of this Jesus People USA event.

That night, in the few hours of sleep I caught between the heat in the camper and the nearly all-night music, I dreamed of that writing class. The teacher in the dream opened with a question. "What's the first task for a writer?"

I raised my hand. "Thinking. Writers are first thinkers."

"Yes, that's good," the teacher said. "Writing is thinking on the page."

Sweat running down my chest woke me. Writing. I'm dreaming about writing! Pulling on my sundress, I climbed out of the Volkswagen van. Maybe a walk would help cool me off, or I could douse myself with the hose, as I'd done in the heat of the afternoon. Our group slept mostly in tents, though a couple of boys slept on cots, open-air. Along the road towards the lake, a few tents sheltered groups of tattooed teenagers, talking quietly. Circling a campfire, a group laid hands on a spiky-haired girl crying softly. Overhead, the stars pierced the night like pinpricks of glory.

I'd often thought of writing my story of triumph over my difficult childhood, but it seemed beyond me. I could not imagine myself a writer. Writers were better thinkers than I was. And yet, before God made me a psychotherapist, I couldn't have imagined myself as a counselor, either. But God gave me the vision, and I finished graduate school ten years ago.

The first time I'd imagined myself a therapist was the day in the early '80s when the psychologist had said, "You're a clinician." Was tonight's dream, where I identified with a professional writer, from God? Was God now saying, "You're a writer?" I gazed at the moonlight reflected across the lake's soft waves. I whispered: "Jesus, what's your plan? I belong to you. Show me the way."

Walking back up the hill toward the food court, I doused myself with the water hose. In the coolness of my wet sundress, I fell asleep in the van until the sun came up.

Back at home the next day, lying on the navy couch where I usually wrote in my journal, a poem idea floated into my mind. I wrote three that day. Within a week, I had written a dozen.

Three weeks later, heart racing, breathing shallowly, I pulled out my first two poems to read to Sheila, formerly an English teacher. In weekly visits, we'd shared our hearts and our lives now for many years. We sat on the back deck, under the ceiling fan. When I read the first one, she cried. After the second, she said, "It's wonderful."

I fell against the seat back. Her response instantly calmed my adrenalin. But another question pushed through.

"Where am I going with this?"

"Don't worry about that. Just get it down and see what you have," she said.

"I feel like Abraham, being asked to leave everything he knows and 'go to a land God will show him,'" I said. "Your response, though, is a great encouragement. Thanks."

From that small encouragement, through a steep multiyear learning curve, my words have been published in national magazines. Those flowers of writing and speaking grow in the rich soil of God's love, shed abroad in my heart. As Papa-God has fathered me in these new identities, his love has continued to devour my shame and strengthen my self-esteem. I saw a new depth of emotional stability in an incident in July of 2007 . . . .

"Hey, get off the blacktop!" yelled the guys applying the sealant to the church parking lot that hot July day. Moments before, I'd realized I'd really screwed up by bicycling through the orange cones at the entrance. In the early nineties, during my struggle with work anxiety, I'd gained forty pounds, but since I'd lost that weight in 2004, I'd been biking everywhere. Because the lot at Vineyard is so big, I thought I could ride through the dried areas. Their anger blew me toward the uncoated half on the other side of the building. We had recently begun attending The Vineyard, where my old friend Don was a pastor and a newspaper columnist.

You weren't thinking. As I locked up my bike, I wiped a tear. Self-absorption doesn't mean worthlessness. Yes, you shouldn't have crossed the cones blocking the entrance. That was a little arrogant. But you're forgivable.

"Is this the entrance?" A woman carrying books at the bottom of the outside stairs interrupted my self-talk.

"Yeah, but I'm not sure it'll be open on this side, though, during the week." We climbed the stairs. The door yielded to my tug.

"Oh, it is." I smiled at her as she took the books to the bookstore while I walked through the expansive lobby to the center reception area.

"Hi Deb, I'm here to see Don." I'd been meeting with Don every other month for a couple of years to talk about writing.

"I'll page him. How are you?" Deb, though a busy receptionist for the church of more than 2000, was always friendly.

"I'm good. Just puttering along. Reading and writing. How about you?"

We chatted for a few minutes before my appointment. Even during the hour-long chat with Don about writing, I didn't mention my wrong turn into the parking lot. Biking home that day, I thought how far God had brought me. Even ten years ago, that reprimand would have brought a gush of tears. I'd have joked about my self-absorption with both Deb and Don, looking for reassurance.

Now, even when I sin, my anchor holds. I am rooted in the compassion and care of a good Father, seeking to maintain the humility in which his seeds can grow. Andrew Murray has said that humility is "honesty with God and hunger for God." We can be honest with God, even saying, "I hate you!" if we also hunger for God, saying, "Clean me out, Lord. Fill me up."

God cleans and clears our ground, pulling the weeds. Then he fills our ground with his seed. And he gives us new experiences to overshadow the memory of old pain. When in 2002 a friend suggested going to Kansas City to a conference at the International House of Prayer, I could only cry tears of joy. That year was twenty-five years since those terrible days in Kansas City when I thought God was throwing me away. At the 2002 meetings, I had a precious time of meeting God in prayer and prophecy. And now the keepsake of Kansas City is not a delusion of destruction but words of comfort from Papa-God.

As I have allowed him to cultivate the wild soil of my heart, Papa has grown more abundance than I ever imagined possible. Again, Charles Greenaway comes to mind, standing in the front of the UAG congregation in the late seventies. "Our God can, our God will, and, if not, he has something better." I was not thrown away to wander the backside of a fiery desert. I live under the oak of God's acceptance, surrounded by lilies of his love.

Of course, my heart still grows weeds. But there's less room for them. The truth of God's compassionate and gracious heart, slow to anger and abounding in love, keeps the lies from rooting. The deepest lie I believed was that God is either all-loving or all-powerful, but he cannot be both. I now cling to the idea that he displays his absolute, all-loving power, not in a continual rescue, but in a constant suffering. In these days between Jesus' first advent and his second coming, God suffers with us to accomplish his purposes.

Our responsibility is to fight the battles with him. He can and will redeem our days if we grieve our losses, forgive the sin against us, fight Satan's lies with God's truth, and trade our earthly fathers for our Forever Father. These are true battles, and Papa-God means to give us true victories.

My biological father was a hardhearted, soft-willed creator of a fiefdom under which I suffered for no good thing. Our Forever Father is a kindhearted, iron-willed creator of a world in which he suffers with us for a coming Kingdom worth everything it costs. Let's not give up fighting these costly battles. Let's believe our Father wants to give us more than we can imagine and that his best is yet to be.

QUESTIONS FOR PERSONAL OR GROUP STUDY

Healing from abuse, grieving our childhood losses, and understanding that God is different from our difficult fathers is a long process, but a journey worth what it costs. Reflecting on these questions either individually or with a group will assist your healing process.

Chapter 1

1. Before visiting her parents, Karen prayed for God's light to shine in the darkness. What is visiting your parents like for you?

2. Karen recounts two memories that show her father's confusing two-sided nature. Has your father's behavior ever confused you? How? How have you dealt with that confusion?

3. Did your father abuse you? Sexually, physically, emotionally, or by neglect? Have you labeled these behaviors "sin"?

Chapter 2

1. Karen says the first rule of dysfunctional families is "don't talk about the real issues." Does your family avoid certain topics? What would happen if you brought them up?
2. Karen felt her father's communication as "crazy-making." Do you see why? Have you ever felt so completely confused by your father that it took you a while to sort it out?
3. Describe your relationship with your father. Close or distant? Safe or treacherous? Was he there? When you were a child, did he provide, protect, confront, and comfort you? Did he do well in one area but fail in other areas?

Chapter 3

1. When she embarrassed herself by wetting her pants in class, Karen's first grade teacher comforted and provided for her. Did teachers help you when you felt ashamed, or did they add to your pain?
2. If we've been deeply hurt, we often find ourselves hurting others, at least in our fantasies, as in Karen's fantasy of spanking her schoolmates. What kind of revenge have you imagined?

3. Emotional neglect is hard to pin down because it's the absence of something that should be there. After she fell off the corn crib, Karen needed comfort. Do you remember times when you needed comfort but didn't get it?

Chapter 4

1. As a little girl, Karen kept the family secret of incest. Did you keep secrets growing up? Maybe incest, or alcoholism, or physical beatings or emotional bullying. Have you talked to God about them? Can you?

2. In spite of the incest, Karen's family functioned very well in many ways. How well did your family take care of the ordinary business of everyday life—cooking, cleaning, eating, and participating in the community? Were you aware of any unresolved tension?

3. Karen says "the two bright spots of my early life were school and sewing." Was school a hard place or a safe place for you? Have hobbies been a means of grace to you? Explain.

Chapter 5

1. Karen describes her first, mismatched romantic relationship with Roger. What was your first relationship like?

2. Karen used sex to feel powerful and to dull her pain. What's been your relationship with your sexuality?

3. The trip to the theatre workshop in upstate New York opened Karen's eyes in many ways. Think about a trip you've taken that has been eye-opening.

Chapter 6

1. Karen's life began to feel meaningless. Have you ever felt your life wasn't going anywhere? How have you found meaning?

2. Why would Karen be willing to hang out with drug addicts? Have you ever done stupid things like that? Do you understand what motivated the behavior?

3. Karen nearly sabotaged the best relationship in her life when she told Jerry she was a prostitute. Have you ever screwed up a relationship? Do you know where that behavior came from?

Chapter 7

1. Karen really did begin a new phase when she moved into the room with Mercedes and Cindy. How has God begun new phases in your life?

2. Karen almost lost the relationship with Jerry because of her controlling nature. Do others

seem to think you can be too bossy? What motivates you to be bossy?

3. The intellectual key to faith, for Karen, was grasping Jesus' continuing life. If you're a believer, was there a key insight that made belief possible?

Chapter 8

1. Did you, or do you know someone, who, like Karen, has gotten depressed or even psychotic after childbirth? What was that like for you or your friend?

2. Karen received a great deal of social and spiritual support during this difficult time. How has God provided for your needs during emotional crises?

3. In the intense stress of the breakdown, Karen began to talk about the previously buried abuse. Has stress also affected you like this, bringing to mind old pains?

Chapter 9

1. After recovery from the postpartum crisis, Karen was sure God had healed her. However, she had another breakdown two years later. Have you ever been prematurely convinced of God's healing? Explain.

2. Why didn't Karen realize she was in trouble again? Have you ever disbelieved something was happening to you because you didn't believe it could happen again?

3. Karen says forgiving her father was crucial to her healing. Have you found forgiveness to be an important component of healing?

Chapter 10

1. The chapter opens with a scene that shows Karen's jealousy of her daughter. How have you felt jealous? What have you done with your jealousy?

2. Karen talks about the "three revelations" of God. What are they? Does this idea make sense to you?

3. Has Father-God revealed his love to you? Maybe not in a powerful experience like Karen had, but over time, so you know in your gut that he is for you? If not, maybe you'd like to pray, "Lord, please reveal the love of the Father to me." Don't stop praying until you know, without a doubt, that God loves you.

Chapter 11

1. Karen owes her sanity to the fellowship at UAG, especially Irene and the Prayer and Share

women. Do you have a group of people who do/
will/would support you through crisis?

2. Karen prayed to see where God was when she
   was being abused. God gave her the image of
   Jesus holding them, weeping. What does that
   image mean to you? Has God comforted you
   with an image or a thought regarding any abuse
   you've experienced?

3. Karen recounts two recurrent childhood dreams
   that typified the emotional atmosphere of her
   childhood. Do you recall any repetitive childhood dreams? What do they say about your
   childhood?

Chapter 12

1. Karen writes: "I often questioned God's involvement when things didn't go my way." Do you
   wonder where God is when life doesn't work out
   the way you want it to? How do you deal with
   these thoughts?

2. God used a "chance" meeting with old friends
   to help her get the university job. How has God
   shown up in unexpected ways to help you?

3. How did the hospital stay show Karen's distrust?
   What experiences in your life have shown you
   your distrust?

Chapter 13

1. Karen admits to physical abuse of her daughter. Have you ever felt that out of control? How have you handled that?
2. Karen feels she has to fight with her daughter over her school work. How could Karen have handled homework issues differently?
3. What do you think about Karen's statement: "Free will costs too much"?

Chapter 14

1. God encouraged Karen about her clinical gifts in several ways: through the psychologist who affirmed her insights, through Barbara's affirmation after being with Loretta in the hospital, and through the house church leadership. How has God affirmed your gifts?
2. Actually doing therapy, though, was harder than Karen anticipated. How did she react? How have you reacted when something is harder than you expected?
3. The last affirmations Karen describes in this chapter are from her superiors. How have good words from your boss affected you? If you're a supervisor, how do you think your good words affect those who report to you?

Chapter 15

1. Karen prayed for understanding about her anger. Have you ever prayed to understand an emotion? What happened?
2. Fear of rejection is a core issue in Karen's anger, going back to the deep fear implanted by the abuse. Almost everyone fears rejection to some extent. How do you respond when you feel rejected?
3. Karen says Satan's lie is "Something is wrong with you; that's why you were abused." Does that make sense to you? How?

Chapter 16

1. In her journal entry, Karen writes of "expecting evil." Do you expect evil? How can we "expect good"?
2. The healing of memories prayer time was very powerful, allowing Karen to realize that God wanted her. How have you sought healing for painful memories?
3. After a family wedding, Karen "trades fathers." Have you, too, needed to let God be your real father? How did your father portray an inadequate picture of God's fatherhood?

Chapter 17

1. After years of working on forgiving her father, Karen still hates him. Have you ever hated someone? How long did it take to deal with that feeling?
2. Karen writes a prayer in her journal: "I don't want to manage this stuff, I want to be delivered!" Are you managing your residual childhood baggage, or is God delivering you? Which do you want?
3. "More and more I leaned on God's heart." When Karen didn't understand God's work, she learned to trust his heart. What helped her do that? What helps you do that?

Chapter 18

1. After viewing *The Mission,* Karen boldly asks for God to speak to her in a dream. Describe a time when you were bold with God. What was the result?
2. At her parents' party in the church basement, Karen could see the space with new eyes, recalling not just the pain, but also God's provision. If you had a difficult childhood, how did God also provide some good experiences and people for you?
3. Finally, Karen confronted her father about the abuse, hoping to develop a more honest

relationship. If you've confronted your father or mother, what motivated it? If you haven't, what might motivate you to confront? When is it a bad idea to confront an abuser?

Chapter 19

1. God tests us to know what is in our hearts (Deut 8:2). What did Karen find in her heart as she drove across town, not knowing whether Jerry was dead or alive? Have you ever been surprised to see what was in your heart, either good or bad?

2. Jerry saw the strength in Karen during this crisis. Sometimes stressful times show us just how strong we are. Has that happened to you? How?

3. The "Letter to Annie" expresses Karen's core understanding of how God feels about our pain. What thoughts does the letter spark for you?

Chapter 20

1. On what basis does Karen imagine her father in heaven? Do you agree?

2. "Satan does not grow flowers," Karen says. What does Satan want to grow? What are some examples, from the book, of weed-lies that Satan grows in Karen's life? What lies have you believed?

3. "He can and will redeem our days if we grieve our losses, forgive the sin against us, fight Satan's lies with God's truth, and trade our earthly fathers for our Forever Father." Where are you in that process?

ENDNOTES

1. Thornton Wilder, *Our Town* (New York: Harper Perennial Modern Classics, 2003), 108.
2. Philip Yancey, *Where is God When It Hurts?* (Grand Rapids: Zondervan, 1977).
3. Peter Kreeft, *Fundamentals of the Faith* (San Francisco: Ignatius Press, 1988), 183.
4. M. Scott Peck, *The Road Less Traveled* (New York: Simon and Schuster, 1978), 76.
5. Lionel Whiston, *Are You Fun to Live With?* (Waco: Word, 1973).
6. Leslie Weatherhead, *When the Lamp Flickers* (New York: Abingdon-Cokesbury Press, 1948), 142.